PROTECTING AND SAFEGUARDING CHILDREN IN SCHOOLS

A Multi-Agency Approach

Mary Baginsky, Jenny Driscoll, Carl Purcell, Jill Manthorpe and Ben Hickman

With a foreword by
Tim Brighouse

P

First published in Great Britain in 2022 by

Policy Press, an imprint of
Bristol University Press
University of Bristol
1-9 Old Park Hill
Bristol
BS2 8BB
UK
t: +44 (0)117 374 6645
e: bup-info@bristol.ac.uk

Details of international sales and distribution partners are available at
policy.bristoluniversitypress.co.uk

British Library Cataloguing in Publication Data
A catalogue record for this book is available from the British Library

ISBN 978-1-4473-5826-8 hardcover
ISBN 978-1-4473-5827-5 paperback
ISBN 978-1-4473-5828-2 ePub
ISBN 978-1-4473-5829-9 ePdf

Cover design: Robin Hawes
Front cover image: iStock/Qweek

Contents

List of figures, tables and boxes

Figures

Tables

Box

Acknowledgements

Most of this book is based on research which we conducted between 2017 and 2019. It was funded by the Economic and Social Research Council to whom we are extremely grateful. Throughout the research we were fortunate to have had an advisory group, the members of which not only attended meetings, but also gave us the benefit of their experience and skills in relation to specific parts of the project and methodology. This group consisted of Professor Anne Edwards (Chair), Edith Badgie, Samantha Clayton, Sir Paul Ennals, Carolyn Eyre, Matthew Gibson, Sonja Hall, Emma-Louise Hodgson, Michelle Lloyd, Georgina Burns-O'Connell, Professor Nigel Parton, Martin Pratt, Katie Rigg, Joycelyn Thompson and Richard White. We were also fortunate to be able to work with Dr Philip Green of the University of Tennessee, who supported our use of the Organisational Social Context Measure.

We are also grateful to Professor Anne Edwards, Dr Susannah Wright and Dr Alun Rees for providing their reflections on sections of the book and to Sir Tim Brighouse for his considered and stimulating Foreword. Isobel Bainton, our link with Policy Press for most of the process, provided consistent and much-welcomed support throughout.

We would never have made it through our schools' case studies without the assistance of our colleague Danielle Clark-Bryan who supported the interviews in schools. Janet Robinson provided administrative support as efficiently as always and Ann Banks dealt with an extraordinary number of transcripts with speed, accuracy and good humour.

We should like to thank the many others who cooperated with us during those two years. We always gave an assurance of confidentiality and anonymity, which means we are not able to name them. In the initial scoping stage we spoke to many individuals from education, children's social care, local authorities' administrative services, specialist services and national agencies, who shared their experience and expertise, which, in turn, helped us to shape the later stages of the project. An important part of the methodology involved surveys that were sent to education services, children's social care and local safeguarding children's boards in every English local authority. The fact that these surveys received a high response rate is due to the significance which individuals in all three agencies attached to the subject and their willingness to transfer this interest into painstakingly complete surveys. The information which they provided not only allowed us to construct a national picture of how they were working with schools to safeguard children, it also enabled us to select a representative group of areas in which we conducted the case studies.

The case studies were based in five local authorities and one academy trust. We are so thankful to all six organisations for the way in which they were willing to consider the request in the first place and then welcome and provide support for this stage. We then worked with 58 schools across the local authorities and trust. We spent a day in all 58 schools, where staff found time to meet with us on top of their many other duties, even giving up free periods and lunchtime to do so. Without their willingness to share their experiences in an open and very honest way this research would have been the poorer.

As authors we hope that we have done justice to the efforts of so many.

Foreword

Tim Brighouse

Everyone is familiar with the African saying that 'It takes a whole village to raise a child'. As we know, it implies that it takes all members of a tightly knit community, in an identifiable and familiar place, to contribute to and be supportive of the individual family in bringing up an infant through childhood and adolescence to adulthood.

Those of us in the publicly funded education, health and social services refer to it often as we seek to overcome the dangerous anonymity which the industrial age brought to what had been for centuries a mainly agricultural society. Most of us are also conscious that technology and digitalisation when applied to communication and the world of work has meant the weakening of the community of 'place' as the various vital people in the community are able almost effortlessly to belong to communities which are not rooted in the place where they live. Such people can survive and thrive without much interaction with the 'place' they happen to be. That is not the case for everyone in their community however, especially those who are either poorer, old, disabled in some way or some combination of all three. Additionally, the clubs, community groups and other facilities and organisations which hold a village together have weakened in some though not all communities. Where that has occurred, the concept of the 'village' helping the hard-pressed family bring up their child is far-fetched, especially if one or other a parent or both are stuck feeling isolated in 'place' or, if in work, sometimes are leaving the immediate 'place' to work long hours on low wages to survive. They are often female and bringing up children alone.

This important book is based on forensic case study research into how far multi-agency work has over time helped those families. The pages shine a bright light on the variable efficacy of multi-agency working in its vital task of helping our most vulnerable children and their families to overcome the formidable obstacles which circumstances have often put in the way of their progress towards living a fulfilled life. You could argue that the concept of the 'village' also applies to this group of professionals within these agencies, whether predominantly teachers, health and social workers, and sometimes colleagues from the police and housing. Their task, as a 'professional village', if brought together in time, is to create fences at the top of the cliff so that the infant, child or adolescent doesn't tumble over the edge. If they fall, all that the professional village can do is to behave like an ambulance at the cliff's base and hope to help the victims to a sanctuary where the professionals exert long, painful, and increasingly desperate effort to try to put 'humpty-dumpty together again'. It is long and expensive repair work which too often emulates the failed outcome of 'all the king's horses and all the king's men' in the nursery rhyme.

Multi-professional/interagency working, as this book reminds us, has a long stuttering history of so many well-intentioned starts and subsequent changes of direction, often caused by their work being at the periphery of one or other of the agencies (Health, Education or Social Care) involved. You understand why it so often ended in tears. Different professional cultures, differing priorities, misunderstandings of meanings, obstacles to data sharing, a failure to understand the basics of and establish protocols for partnership working – all have undermined the best of intentions.

That does not mean that it is as easy to forgive the failures of national leadership which have caused multi-agency work to falter.

There are two points in the story where one sees vivid and contrasting examples of the impact of national leadership at the highest level affecting multi-agency working and the vulnerable young people the professionals from different disciplines seek to help. Each example concerns the launch of new policy.

The first of the two contrasting examples affecting multi agency working was the occasion of the energetic development of Every Child Matters (ECM) agenda within the renamed Department of Children Schools and Families (previously the variously named Department of/(for) Education/(& Skills)/(& Business) when Ed Balls was Secretary of State. The day after the launch, Ed Balls arrived at the newly renamed Department to find civil servants busy taking down the rainbow placards and other symbolic paraphernalia of the previous day's launch and Balls immediately told the workers to stop and put them back up. 'This wasn't simply for a day' he declared 'It is a permanent change'.

The second example concerns a second launch at the same place. Shift the clock forward to 2010 and the first act of Michael Gove as Ed Balls' successor was, as recorded in this book, to rename the Department as 'for Education' and remove the rainbow and associated display. Even more importantly he changed priorities and the language which had been used to underpin the ECM agenda.

Each involved policy launches. One of the problems of government departments is that they love the publicity which goes with the launch of a new policy. There is a temporary feel-good factor which provides a momentary fillip to those, whose daily round is more usually occupied with crisis and complexity. While they are good at launches, they are less good at is attending to the subtleties of introducing the launched policy effectively in all its complex stages and different settings across the country. Much more likely is that their attention moves to other things. That's why there are so many new policy launches and so few boats which arrive at their intended ports. This is sadly illustrated in this book.

It comes out just after the launch of another attempt at multi-agency working. It will therefore be timely for those involved to read this book to avoid the pitfalls of the past and deal effectively with the complexities of the present. This time it is led by the NHS through the gradual development of the Integrated Care Systems (ICS) which are intended to be wider in scope than the focus of this book but also fashioned to suit the varying contexts of different local communities.

And that is where we come to some of the complexities of the present. There are two principal partners to those in the NHS: on the one hand Local Government, reflective of those different contexts, and home to social workers and on the other, those working in educational setting mainly teachers in schools. While local government, despite a decade of the deepest cuts to expenditure ever experienced, will be energetic in embracing ICS colleagues, it is less clear that those in education will be similarly enthusiastic.

Consider what is happening in the schooling system where young people spend most of their time not spent either at home or in the community. It is arguable that there are 'toxins' in the schooling system which are contributing to the failure of what the Newsom Report called 'Half Our Future' as long ago as 1968 or what Geoff Barton the General Secretary of the Association of School and College Leaders (ASCL) last year called 'the forgotten third' of pupils who emerge with very little benefit from their school experiences. Included in that proportion of children are very likely the more than 7,500 each year permanently excluded from our schools. In Scotland our close neighbour and a tenth the size of England, there are not 750 (a tenth) excluded each year, nor even 75 (a hundredth) but 5. English schools have become one of the most likely to exclude among those in the western world.

Part of the reason is the difference in approaches to behaviour within the two countries' schools. In England in the last decade many schools have adopted what is sometimes called 'assertive discipline' or 'zero tolerance' approaches backed by a Behaviour Tsar at the DfE. In Scotland through a variety of measures, a much more positive approach has begun to pay dividends.

It was not always so and it is worth speculating why, especially if we are anxious to reduce the case load of those trying to make a fist of multi-agency working. We certainly can't afford schools creating slippery paths at the top of the cliff.

During the years of austerity since 2010, the English schooling system has marched to a different set of tunes. It was not merely the symbolic act of the incoming Michael Gove, referred to in the body of this book and mentioned above, it was also the impact of other policies. The curriculum has narrowed and become more slanted towards the academic: so, for example, drama, music, and the arts generally have had less time. Examinations and tests are taken not when children are ready to pass them but at the same age and time of the year for every pupil in order to serve a fierce school accountability regime. Moreover, for the same reasons perhaps, exams and tests are norm-referenced so that there is an assured failure percentage irrespective of standards. Recently the cumulative collective pupil GCSE outcomes over eight subjects have been compared with the same pupils' performance at age 11 to give what is called Progress 8 school league tables. These are organised around an average meaning that as many schools are above as below average. Schools themselves have become Academies as though that in itself will ensure school improvement. Once they are academies, they can more or less ignore their local authority, and some do so far as admissions and exclusions of challenging pupils are concerned.

Amid such competitive influences it is unsurprising that more children feel they do not fit in and that schooling is not for them.

In the years of austerity, it isn't simply that multi-agency working (affecting vulnerable children adolescents and their families) has necessarily defaulted to work in ambulances at the bottom of the cliff. Far more seriously it seems that some of those working at the top are creating arrangements which make it more likely that children and adolescents find themselves tottering on the cliff edge.

There are signs – various Education Commissions including one sponsored by *The Times* newspaper – that we are at one of those periods of change such as occurred at the end of the Second World War and again in the 1980s – when the nation is about to draw breath and move towards a new age for schooling. The Butler Act of 1944 ushered in an age of *Trust and Optimism* (albeit slightly uncritical and misplaced) which opened up opportunities for the most able few among the poor. Baker's 1988 Act created an age of *Markets, Centralisation and Managerialism* which has brought its successes for the many. But there is still a third of pupils excluded from enjoying their education and therefore the likelihood of growing up fulfilled citizens committed to the fulfilment of others. Just maybe the outcomes of the Commissions and the debate they are causing will herald a new age of *Hope Ambition and Collaborative Partnerships*.

Whether it does or not, there will always be pupils whose needs are so great that they need timely interdisciplinary work from multi-agency partnerships.

The lessons in this book will be an invaluable guide to those agencies and their workers committed to making better the lives of those who are in the most need.

Introduction

1

Making sense of schools' engagement in multi-agency working in the changed educational landscape

Introduction

This book aims to provide readers with a deeper and contemporary understanding of the role that schools are playing as part of the multi-agency response to child protection and safeguarding in England. It draws on a research project that was funded by the Economic and Social Research Council in which we talked to over 300 people, including school staff, social workers and experts in child safeguarding policy and practice, with many more responding to surveys. It places this investigation within the historical, policy and political realities that impact on schools and the agencies with which they work. This book is not a guide to how people working in schools and other agencies should work together to protect and safeguard children. Rather, it describes how people in schools and other agencies do work together to protect and safeguard children and how this work might be improved.

Collaborative practice to protect children from harm was promoted by the Children Act 1989, one of the intentions of which was to reduce compulsory intervention in families' lives by promoting more supportive partnership with families whose children were identified as being 'in need'. The first roadmap to this Act was in the form of the 1991 statutory guidance *Working Together Under the Children Act 1989: A Guide to the Arrangements for Inter-Agency Cooperation for the Protection of Children from Abuse* (Home Office et al, 1991). This set out how the Act was to be interpreted. As Parton and Berridge (2011) remarked, by the time the next version of this document appeared in 1999 it had not only undergone a substantial rewrite, but it had also acquired a new title. The reference to abuse was dropped and it became *Working Together to Safeguard Children: Inter-Agency Working to Safeguard and Promote the Welfare of Children* (Department of Health et al, 1999). This terminology reflects the emerging view of this area of work as a continuum from parental support at one end to child protection at the other, which underpinned Lord Laming's proposals in response to the Victoria Climbié inquiry (Laming, 2003) and the Children Act 2004. This Act, together with the *Every Child Matters* (ECM) programme (HM Government, 2003), which applied to the well-being of children and young people, required a range of professionals not only to work together to manage the protection of children, but also to engage with the broader safeguarding agenda, tackle social exclusion and promote the welfare of all children (see Parton, 2016). The 2006 version of the *Working Together* guidance (HM Government, 2006) defined what 'safeguarding' covered. The concept brought together protection from abuse, the prevention of damage to health and development, and the promotion of those conditions that would improve children's life chances.

This chapter provides background on the rationale for the research and outlines the methodologies used at each stage, as well as setting the context for subjects explored in later chapters. The research took place between 2017 and 2019 and, while some work was conducted with other agencies, our focus was on schools. There were sound reasons for this. It is widely recognised that schools are in a good position to identify abuse and neglect because school staff see children nearly every day in term time and so they are often able to recognise any changes, be they good or bad. As a result, schools and education services are an important source for the identification and referral of child protection concerns, accounting for 20 per cent of all referrals to local children's services in the year to 31 March 2020 (Department for Education (DfE), 2020a) compared with 29 per cent from the police and 15 per cent from the NHS.[1] This is a substantial increase since 2014, when the figure for schools and education services was 16 per cent.

While schools are a source of referrals, they are also required to work in partnership with other agencies. Progressively schools have also been brought into a multi-agency response to children's and families' needs and, in some instances, are charged with the task of coordinating support to families. While there is a vast literature on multi-agency work, much of which identifies facilitators and barriers, there is very limited empirical research on how it translates into service delivery or outcomes (Daniel et al, 2011; Baginsky, 2018). We set out to examine the role of schools within the kaleidoscopic world of child protection through the lens of the increased autonomy granted to all schools over the past 20 years, largely through the extension of the Academies programme and the greater independence of all schools. Our study focused on England alone because of the extent to which policy and practice in child protection and safeguarding in the four UK nations have diverged in recent years, as well as pre-existing differences in education systems. In particular, none of the three other nations have introduced the equivalent to academies so have not experienced the increased complexity in the relationship between schools and local authorities that occurred in England.

Academisation

The Education Act 1944 placed most state-funded schools, generically known as state schools, under the control of local authorities. However, since the 1980s successive governments have pushed to give schools greater control over education spending and limit the influence of local authorities (Ball, 2021). In 2000 the status of 'academy' was introduced as part of an initiative to drive up educational standards. Schools that were judged by Ofsted[2] to be 'failing' schools were to be closed and replaced by new schools. These were to be publicly funded schools operating independently of local authorities with power to set their own governance arrangements and to disregard certain parts of the national curriculum, allowing them to innovate both in what was taught and how it was taught.

However, this policy, initially implemented under a Labour government to improve struggling schools that were based mainly in deprived areas, was adapted by the Conservative-Liberal Democrat Coalition Government (2010–15) in the Academy Act 2010. Under this government the philosophy driving academisation shifted from a focus on improving failing schools to one emphasising the benefits of greater autonomy for all schools. Following the Academies Act 2010 schools that Ofsted judged to be 'outstanding' could apply to become academies, with substantial financial incentives to do so, but the *Importance of Teaching* White Paper (DfE, 2010) published later that year signalled that this would be extended to 'good' schools (see Purcell, 2020).

Early in 2016 another White Paper *Educational Excellence Everywhere* (DfE, 2016) suggested that all local authority-maintained schools would be forced to become academies by 2022. While the government reversed this in the face of opposition from MPs of all parties and abandoned any intention to use 'force', it maintained its commitment to all schools becoming academies. Speaking at the annual conference of the National Association of Schoolmasters and Union of Women Teachers (NASUWT) the then Secretary of State for Education, Nicky Morgan MP, announced that she would still be introducing new powers which would trigger conversion of all schools in an area if a local authority was underperforming or if it was no longer financially viable for it to run schools. This commitment was reiterated later in the year by Morgan's successor, Justine Greening MP, in a written parliamentary statement (Hansard, 2016). In the intervening time, and several Secretaries of State later, there have been cases of forced academisation, but there have also been reversals of notices in the light of parental opposition and improved Ofsted gradings (Allen-Kinross, 2019). Yet in 2021 the then Secretary of State, Gavin Williamson (2021) MP, speaking at the Confederation of School Trusts, stated the government's goal remained for all schools to join an academy trust.

Crin (2014) found no one *dominant* reason why schools chose to convert to academies. The most frequently cited reason was associated with a desire to raise attainment, followed by financial gain and then the desire to have greater control over that funding. At the start of 2005 there were 17 academies and a further 35 were planned. According to the National Audit Office (NAO)

(2018a), by early 2018, when our research had just got underway, 7,472 of the 21,538 state-funded schools in England were academies. They made up 27 per cent of primary schools and 72 per cent of secondary schools. The NAO concluded that most local authority areas were likely to continue to have both academies and maintained schools for the foreseeable future, but it recognised that the disparity between the primary and secondary sectors made it difficult for local authorities to adopt an integrated approach to children's education. The NAO also found that the proportion of schools that were academies varied widely across England, from 93 per cent in the London Borough of Bromley to 6 per cent in Lancashire, the London Borough of Lewisham and North Tyneside.

This is significant because important responsibilities are conferred on local authorities under the Children Act 1989 to protect children from harm and promote the welfare of children in need of additional support. These were supplemented by section 10 of the Children Act 2004, which makes local authorities responsible for promoting cooperation across the relevant agencies to improve the welfare of all children. These duties are not restricted to children who attend local authority-maintained schools or to agencies that they support. This means that while local authorities have a legal duty to keep all children safe from harm and to promote their welfare, the way they operate has had to change in the context of a far more autonomous school system.

Although the government directs all schools to continue to maintain a strong relationship with local authorities, it was left to individual schools to determine the form of that relationship (Department for Education, 2010). Thus, while government policy pushed the greater detachment of schools and local authorities, the question of how their statutory safeguarding responsibilities were to be fulfilled was largely absent from the debate that took place at that time. A House of Commons Committee of Public Accounts (2015) report said that local authorities' ability to fulfil their statutory responsibilities was 'undermined' in areas where high proportions of schools had become academies. The report referred to a NAO survey (NAO, 2014a) which showed that 13 of the 87 local authorities surveyed did not monitor academies' safeguarding arrangements and 13 also indicated they would not intervene directly in an academy if pupil safety was threatened. The study reported throughout this book provided the opportunity to examine what, if any, the implications of academisation had been for schools and local authorities as far as child protection and safeguarding were concerned.

Multi-agency work with children and families

Very soon after embarking on any literature review or examination of multi-agency working a reader will encounter what Leathard (1994) labelled a 'terminological quagmire' (p 5) with the confusion and overlaps that exist around the various terms. There are those who have attempted to draw a distinction between them, for example Wilson and Pirrie (2000) and others such as Atkinson et al (2005), who developed typologies of practice. However, we followed the lead of Tomlinson (2003) and Jones and Leverett (2008), who are, among others, happy to use 'multi-agency', 'inter-agency', 'interdisciplinary' and 'joint' working to reflect any collaborative relationships. We have used 'multi-agency' to cover all communication and negotiation between professionals, occupations, agencies and disciplines; we equated multi-agency with any situations where agencies worked or aspired to work together. This interpretation allowed us to explore the strategic and operational manifestations of multi-agency work, including different types of approaches with varying structures and methods of coordination.

There is also little consistent evidence on the effectiveness of multi-agency work in general (Cameron and Lart, 2003; Oliver et al, 2010) and involving schools in particular (McDonald et al, 2001; Daniel et al, 2011). Despite this, multi-agency working has become a key policy goal in the UK, across Europe (Barnes and Melhuish, 2017; Baginsky, 2018) and elsewhere (Friedman et al, 2007; Statham, 2011). It has been a major driver of policy development in children's services for over half a century, with evidence that the concept was influential well before that. Whatever term is used, service integration and collaboration have a developed theoretical history of their own. Halpern (1991), Kahn and Kamerman (1992) and Kagan (1993) have all traced integrated service delivery in the United States (US) back to the 19th century. The Charitable Organisation Societies (COS) that spread across the US in the latter half of that century attempted to coordinate the work of the numerous small charities. They set up central registers and held 'case conferences' to bring together the different agencies working with specific families to maximise efficient use of resources but also to counter families receiving relief from more than one source. Cox and Garvin (1970) provide an excellent analysis of how these initiatives developed into the structures that underpinned US social welfare until the middle of the 20th century.

In England Spiker (2000) has explored how the 'new' Poor Law, introduced in the 1830s, saw healthcare providers and embryonic social services organisations working together to address poverty, also helped, as in the US, by charitable organisations. From the middle of the 19th century social reformers focused more attention on children's education and welfare and took steps to begin to address the extremely poor conditions experienced by so many. However, the centrality of collaboration developed during the last century gained new momentum in the UK during the 1960s and 1970s. It was officially recognised in several reports, including the Plowden Report (Central Advisory Council for Education, 1967) and the Seebohm Committee Report (1968). Chapter 2 explores this period in more detail but in the years that followed it became clear how hard it was to translate a vision and guidance into reality. Inquiries into child deaths at the hands of those who had abused or neglected them recorded instances of missed opportunities by professionals to share vital information. The Children Act 1989 placed 'interagency working at the heart of the remit for social services' (Anning et al, 2006, p 5) in order to produce a more efficient and effective service for children, young people and their families and promote a more concerted attempt to develop systematic strategies and programmes. However, Leiba and Weinstein (2003) have perceptively argued that it is easier to identify the harms arising from breakdown in communication between agencies than to demonstrate that inter-agency collaboration prevents harm.

Examining the contemporary role of schools in multi-agency work

Prior to our research the most detailed examination of schools' engagement in child protection and safeguarding work was conducted between 2002 and 2005 (Baginsky, 2007). This longitudinal study tracked the experiences of staff in 43 schools, across three local authority areas, who had referred cases they were concerned about to children's social care services. When a case was passed to social services, where children's social care was then based, every effort was made to determine what then happened to help understand how the two agencies were viewing the same cases. The report details the progress or otherwise of the referrals, but it is important to note its three key findings regarding the way in which schools and social services worked together.

First, staff shortages and lack of resources were causing social services to struggle to allocate child protection referrals to social workers. Second, the joined-up approach across education and children's social care policy at the national level was not reflected on the ground. *Working Together* (Department of Health (DH) et al, 1999) and the *Framework for the Assessment of Children in Need and their Families* (DH et al, 2000) were supposed to be driving the practice of social work with children and families, but schools were barely aware of these documents and very little training had been provided for teachers. So, when they were asked to contribute to the holistic assessments required by the *Assessment Framework*, teachers complained or felt inadequate and social workers despaired. Schools believed they were being asked to carry out too much investigation before making a referral and many social workers thought schools were making unnecessary demands on their time. And third, although schools said they were committed to playing a significant role in child protection, there were fundamental misunderstandings and too few opportunities to resolve these through discussions at a local level. This undermined multi-agency work, which is dependent on trust and respect being established before any effective work is possible (Intriligator, 1990). The study highlighted the distance that existed between education and social services in terms of their very different professional cultures and the absence of opportunities to develop shared understandings. A study by the Centre for Educational Research and Innovation (1996) of services for children 'at risk' in five countries (Denmark, France, the Netherlands, Sweden and the UK) reached similar conclusions.

Multi-agency safeguarding arrangements

Since this earlier study much has changed both in terms of schools' responsibilities in relation to safeguarding, but also in the multi-agency structures, systems and processes designed to support schools and other agencies to meet these responsibilities. Chapter 2 considers developments over the past two decades as part of a longer discussion on the historical role schools have played in relation to child and family welfare. However, it is important to note here that during the study reported in this book the government introduced new multi-agency safeguarding arrangements (DfE, 2018a) at the local level to replace Local Safeguarding Children Boards (LSCBs), which had been set up in 2006 and which still operated when we began. Under the LSCB arrangements it had been a requirement that schools be represented at this strategic level. However, under the new arrangements only the local authority, the police and health services (represented by NHS Clinical Commissioning Groups) became the 'safeguarding partners' with overall responsibility for ensuring the effectiveness of multi-agency working in relation to child protection and safeguarding. Controversially, schools were given 'relevant agency' status alongside many others and were not therefore placed at the heart of new arrangements as they had been in LSCBs. The development of these new arrangements and the views of research participants on them are considered in Chapter 3.

Austerity and child welfare inequalities

This research was conducted at a time when public services, including schools and children's social care services, were under considerable strain, compounded subsequently by the Coronavirus pandemic. The years since the 2008 financial crisis have been labelled a time of austerity, reflecting the policies introduced by the Conservative-Liberal Democrat Coalition Government (2010–15) and continued by Conservative governments since then. Although overall spending on education has been protected, this spending has not kept pace with rises in pupil numbers. The Institute for Fiscal Studies (Farquharson et al, 2021) reported that spending per pupil in England fell by 9 per cent between 2009/10 and 2019/20, the largest cut in over 40 years. Furthermore, schools serving the most deprived areas have seen the biggest cuts. According to the National Audit Office (2018b) funding allocated to local authorities by central government fell by 49.1 per cent in real terms between 2010/11 and 2017/18. Furthermore, it was also authorities serving the poorest communities that had relied most on this funding and which have seen the biggest cuts (Centre for Cities, 2019). The impact of these cuts has been compounded by cuts to welfare payments that have contributed to rising poverty levels, with 4.2 million children now living in poverty (Joseph Rowntree Foundation, 2021), and of course by the pandemic.

But austerity not only led to major reductions in public spending. It has also been viewed as part of a political project to reshape and reduce the social role of the state (Krugman, 2015; Cummins, 2018). In England this has been reflected in the shift from broad child welfare policies towards a much narrower focus on child protection (Parton, 2014; Purcell, 2020). Spending on 'early intervention' services such as children's centres and youth services fell by almost half (48 per cent) between 2010/11 and 2019/20 (Williams and Franklin, 2021). Furthermore, these reductions have been largest in areas serving the poorest communities – between 2010 and 2019 spending in Walsall, for example, fell by 81 per cent in contrast to much more affluent Surrey, where it fell by only 10 per cent (House of Lords Public Services Committee, 2021).

The impact of austerity policies on the provision of child welfare services in different local authority areas has been closely analysed by contributors to the Child Welfare Inequalities Project (CWIP), funded by the Nuffield Foundation (Bywaters et al, 2016; 2018; 2020; Morris et al, 2018; Webb and Bywaters, 2018). It is difficult to summarise such a comprehensive and complex project. However, as Webb and Bywaters (2018) confirm, budget cuts have been the most severe in the most disadvantaged areas. This disparity is even more glaring when we consider that they also found that children in the most deprived 10 per cent of English neighbourhoods are over 10 times more likely to be in foster or residential care or on protection plans than children in the least deprived 10 per cent. These patterns are partly explained by reductions in central government grants. However, it is also evident that authorities have been forced to cut spending on early intervention or 'preventative' services because more families are judged to be at crisis point, and this is reflected in higher levels of child protection activity over recent years (Hood et al, 2020). Analysis by Bennett et al (2022) found that a 1 per cent increase in child poverty was associated with five additional children entering care per 100,000. Moreover, the CWIP team argued that in many areas dealing with the consequences of deprivation, poverty had become 'the wallpaper of practice ... too big to tackle and too familiar to notice'

(Morris et al, 2018, p 370). It also provided the context within which our research was conceived, developed and conducted.

The research design and process

At the heart of the study reported in this book was an exploration of the structures, arrangements and policies in place at national and local levels to support English schools in fulfilling *their* responsibilities to safeguard and protect children and how they were responding, especially how they were working with other agencies. Two key questions guided the research:

1. How effectively do multi-agency arrangements at local government level support schools in the identification, referral and management of child protection and safeguarding concerns?
2. How do staff in schools make decisions in relation to child protection concerns and what support do they receive to do so?

Given that in 2018 there were over 20,000 schools in England across 150 local authority areas and over 700 multi-academy trusts (MATs),[3] responding to these questions was always going to be a difficult challenge. To explore how schools were managing their responsibilities for child protection and safeguarding in a splintered and diverse environment we adopted a four-stage, multi-level approach to the research to examine the interaction of developments at the local authority and school levels. In summary, the four stages of the research consisted of:

1. a literature review;
2. scoping interviews involving participants in 20 local authorities and national stakeholders;
3. national surveys of local authority education services, children's social care and LSCBs;
4. case studies of schools spread across five local authority areas and one MAT.

In addition to these four key phases of the research we also re-interviewed 12 teachers and 10 social workers who had trained or practised during the 1970s/1980s to inform Chapter 2, which provides a historical perspective on schools' engagement in child protection and safeguarding.

Literature review and scoping interviews

The literature review spanned policy documents, the professional press, and social media as well as research, and informed our scoping interviews with

94 participants. These included 68 professionals working in children's social care or education services in 20 local authorities that were as geographically and demographically representative of England as possible. The remaining 26 individuals included one professional expert involved in safeguarding policy at national level in each of the devolved governments of Northern Ireland, Scotland and Wales. These helped to provide context to our examination of the effect of recent policy changes in England. The other non-local authority participants held knowledge and expertise in specific aspects of safeguarding, including relatively new challenges such as social media use, mental health and anti-social behaviour as well as more traditional factors known to be related to child abuse such as domestic violence and alcohol and substance misuse. The literature review and scoping interviews provided us with a better understanding of the safeguarding challenges schools were facing and were also used to inform our national surveys in the next stage of the project.

National surveys

We designed three related surveys comprising both open and closed questions, which were loaded onto an online platform for completion by representatives of education services, children's social care and LSCBs in all English local authorities. While some questions were included in all three surveys, others were relevant to only one or two of the agencies. We contacted 150 local authority children's services departments[4] to explain the purpose of the surveys and to invite them to select the most appropriate individuals in education and children's social care to complete them. Links to the online survey were subsequently sent out to individuals identified in 125 authorities, after 12 declined to participate owing to resource constraints, and 13 did not respond to repeated contacts. The survey was sent to all 150 LSCBs by the then Association of Independent Chairs of LSCBs. Responses were received from:

- 93 education representatives (62 per cent response rate);
- 80 children's social care representatives (53 per cent response rate);
- 82 LSCBs (55 per cent response rate).

These survey responses provided a rich source of information which complemented and helped to validate the findings of our initial literature review and scoping interviews. The findings of these stages of the research are reported in detail in Chapter 3.

The case studies

The case studies formed the final stage of the study. Case studies can be used to explain, describe or explore events or phenomena in the everyday contexts in which they occur (Yin, 2009). Through in-depth interviews with key members of school staff with safeguarding responsibilities, we sought to examine:

- the extent to which current multi-agency arrangements supported schools in the identification, referral and management of child protection and safeguarding concerns;
- how staff in schools made decisions in relation to child protection concerns and cases;
- how the engagement of schools in local area arrangements for safeguarding children might be strengthened.

To identify five suitable local authority areas where this research would be carried out, we used cluster analysis on the survey data to assess the extent to which the views expressed by the different agencies (education, children's social care and LSCB) in each local area were in alignment. Through this analysis we identified five groups of local authorities categorised on a 'congruence' scale ranging from very high to very low. More detail about this analysis and the analytical techniques we used is reported in Appendix 1.

One area from each of the five 'congruence' groups was then selected for the case studies with the overall aim to arrive at a set of case study areas representing different regions, local authority type and size, and socio-economic context. The names of the five case study areas have been changed to protect anonymity:

- Middle County (very high congruence) is a large local authority in the Midlands with over 200 state-funded schools, of which over 30 per cent were academies at the time this research started in 2017. It is a relatively affluent area and is in the lowest 25 per cent of areas for economic deprivation according to the Index of Multiple Deprivation (Ministry of Housing Communities and Local Government, 2019).
- London Borough (high congruence) is a small local authority with well under 100 schools, of which almost 20 per cent were academies in 2017. It is one of the top 10 per cent most economically disadvantaged areas in England.
- Northern Unitary (medium congruence) is a small local authority with approximately 100 schools, of which over 30 per cent were academies in 2017. It is a middle-ranking authority in terms of economic deprivation, although it includes some neighbourhoods with very high levels of economic deprivation. It is in the top 50 per cent of local authorities for economic disadvantage, but 15 per cent of its lower super output areas were in the top 10 per cent nationally for economic disadvantage.

- Northern City (low congruence) is a large local authority with over 150 schools, of which just under 15 per cent were academies in 2017. It is one of the top 10 per cent most economically disadvantaged areas in England.
- Rural Unitary (very low congruence) is a small local authority in the south-east of England with under 100 schools, of which just over 10 per cent were academies in 2017. It is a very affluent area and is in the bottom 10 per cent of authorities for economic deprivation.

In addition, we also conducted a case study based on schools that were part of a large national MAT with schools located in multiple local authority areas. With the aim of recruiting 10 schools in each area and in the MAT, we distributed a short survey to all state-funded primary, secondary and special schools (generally for children with complex disabilities) in each of the six groups through the local authority and MAT education safeguarding leads. Schools were asked whether they would be happy to be contacted to discuss further participation in the research project. In total 202 schools completed the survey, of which 124 agreed to discuss further participation in the research. Purposive selection was undertaken to include education phases (primary and secondary), local authority-maintained and academy schools and, where possible, one special school in each area, except in the MAT which did not include special schools. We also aimed to reflect different socio-economic conditions (based on free school meals numbers). In total we successfully recruited 58 schools to participate in the research – 10 from each local authority area and eight from the MAT. At the time of the research 28 of the 58 schools had academy status. These included 32 primary schools, 18 secondary schools, two 'all-through schools' and five special schools. The schools included:

- three infant schools (pupils aged 4–7);
- one junior school (pupils aged 7–11);
- 29 primary schools (pupils aged 4–11);
- 18 secondary schools (pupils aged 11–18);
- five special schools (mixed age ranges).

Further detail regarding school type and socio-economic context is included in Appendix 2.

In total 197 interviews involving 213 participants were carried out with key members of staff in schools including the Designated Safeguarding Lead (DSL), head teachers, senior leaders, pastoral staff and school governors. All interviews were digitally recorded, with the participants' consent, and then transcribed. The interview schedule was adaptable for use in one-to-one and group interviews and was segmented into questions for specific roles and general areas. A separate set of questions was designed for governors. The data from these interviews were analysed using thematic analysis (Braun and Clark, 2006), an approach commonly used by qualitative researchers. This was supplemented by use of a technique known as Qualitative Comparative Analysis (QCA), which involves the categorisation and comparison of qualitative data to explore causal relationships between conditions and outcomes (Ragin, 1987; 2000). Where the QCA identified a relationship between an outcome and certain conditions this is highlighted in the chapters that follow. More detail about how this technique was utilised is provided in Appendix 3.

Most participants also completed an Organisational Structural Context (OSC) survey, which is a 105-item survey that seeks to measure the 'cultures and climates' of child welfare and mental health organisations (see Glisson and Green, 2011). This research is one of the few studies to have used the OSC outside the US, where it was developed. We worked with Philip Green of the Center for Behavioral Health Research at the University of Tennessee, where the OSC was developed, to adapt the OSC for use in England by anglicising terms and trialling in five schools for comprehension and applicability. Using the OSC enabled us to produce a profile of the working environment within each school. Findings from the OSC are reported in Appendix 4.

The chapters that follow

The first part of this book focuses on the national picture in relation to schools' involvement in child protection and safeguarding. Sharon Kagan of Columbia University, New York, has examined collaboration across agencies for many years and one of her publications is entitled *Integrating Services for Children and Families; Understanding the Past to Shape the Future* (Kagan, 1993). We have adopted that theme in Chapter 2, where we describe how schools have always played a role in children's lives outside the school day and how, over the years, this has become formalised. Susannah Wright provides an educational historian's reflection on how this role has evolved within a complex terrain where education and social welfare collide. Building on this historical perspective, Chapter 3 provides a contemporary picture that draws on our review of recent literature, the scoping interviews and the national surveys. Anne Edwards reflects on the findings presented in Chapter 3, commenting on how the reality of multi-agency work has changed since the millennium. She concludes that this has not been for the better in a climate where agencies have been subject to budget cuts and, at a policy level, priorities have shifted.

The second part of the book comprises three chapters that draw primarily on the case studies we carried out involving discussions with staff in 58 schools. Chapter 4 reflects on how schools have responded to the challenges they currently face and the broader responsibilities they now have in relation to child protection and safeguarding. Chapter 5 considers schools' experiences of referring cases to children's social care. Following this, Chapter 6 examines what schools told us about cases judged not to meet the threshold for a children's social care intervention but where some form of 'early help' may be needed to support individual children and their families. At the end of this section of the book Alun Rees offers his reflections on the recent experiences of schools.

Finally in Chapter 7 we draw our discussion together and consider, among other things, how schools' role in a multi-agency approach has changed during the first 20 years of the 21st century. Although the substantive research for this book was carried out earlier, a postscript also considers what more recent studies carried out during the COVID-19 pandemic have told us about the impact on schools and partner agencies responsible for the protection and safeguarding of children.

PART I

The national picture

A historical perspective: the evolving role of schools in child protection and safeguarding

Introduction

To understand the role that schools are currently playing in a multi-agency approach to child protection and safeguarding, as well as the facilitators and challenges they face, it helps to understand a little of the journey that has taken them to that role (Kagan, 1993). Surprisingly few people have explored the role of schools in promoting children's welfare in the UK, but it is possible to construct a picture of that journey from different sources, helped also by those who have worked in and for schools and local authorities over the past 30–40 years. The subject is one that deserves a great deal more attention than it has received.

This chapter is organised into five sections. The first section considers the long history of schools as one of the key agencies promoting the welfare of children, stretching back to the mid 19th century, a period of early social reform pre-dating the modern welfare state in industrialised countries. This is followed in the second section by a discussion of key developments from the late 1960s and through to the 1980s. It was during this period that strong evidence emerged that pointed towards the need for schools, alongside other agencies, to play a more central role under multi-agency arrangements to protect children. The landmark Children Act 1989, which continues to provide the main legal framework for child protection and safeguarding, is considered in the third section. Education and welfare reforms introduced under the Labour government (1997–2010) are subsequently discussed in the fourth section. The final section considers research that has examined the roles played by non-teaching welfare professionals based in English schools. The thoughts of Susannah Wright conclude the chapter and a Timeline charting the evolution of schools and children's welfare can be found in Appendix 5.

The long history of schools and child welfare

Crane (2018) has observed that responses to concerns about children and their welfare have ebbed and flowed over the past 150 years, meaning that there have been times of intense interest and action followed by periods when they were seemingly ignored. It was from the middle of the 19th century that social reformers began to pay particular attention to children's education and welfare in an attempt to change the extremely poor conditions experienced by so many people as the UK industrialised. Although there had been earlier attempts to bring elementary education to the poor in England (Cockburn et al, 1969), the Elementary Education Act 1870 made full-time school places available for all children aged 5–12 and the Education Act 1880 introduced compulsory full-time education for that age group. The same Act introduced the role of School Attendance Officers to make sure children attended, with parents facing prosecution if their children failed to do so. Eventually School Attendance Officers became Education Welfare Officers (EWOs) although, as discussed later in this chapter, while there have been times when they assumed wider responsibility for pupils' welfare, their focus has remained on attendance.

Nearly two decades after the 1870 Act, the first UK Act for the Prevention of Cruelty to, and Protection of, Children was passed in 1889, commonly known as the Children's Charter. It is an important marker in the history of childhood in that it recognised that 'children were a class apart from adults requiring specialised legislative intervention' (Walsh, 2020). For the first time it allowed the British state to intervene in the parent–child relationship using legal sanctions. Police officers could arrest anyone found ill-treating a child and remove the child from the family home (Ferguson, 1992). After another 20 years the Children Act 1908 appeared on the statute books, which, while largely concerned with juvenile courts, did introduce the registration of foster parents and, more significantly for this study, gave local authorities powers to keep poor children out of the poorhouse or workhouse and protect them from abuse. The move was not entirely altruistic. It was a response to the perceived threat that unsocialised children posed to society and the economy, and any improvement to their welfare, while welcome, was consequential (Dingwall et al, 1984). In the meantime, the Education Act 1902 replaced School Boards with Local Education Authorities (LEAs), although it was not until the Children and Young Persons Act 1933 that local authorities became responsible for bringing children in need of care and protection to the courts.

Schools are a part of the broad societal landscape and have usually been connected to the communities in which they are based in a variety of ways. The COVID-19 pandemic focused attention on their provision of practical and emotional support beyond their walls (Baginsky and Manthorpe, 2020b; Driscoll et al, 2021), but that was only an extension of what many schools have been doing over many years. Teachers whose pupils live in impoverished conditions know that schooling alone cannot provide the chance for them to thrive.

Their responses to the problems arising from poverty came from a growing understanding that hungry, sick and abused children were not going to able to take advantage of educational opportunities to attain a better life in the future. There are anecdotal accounts and literary mentions of how some Victorian schools provided for children and families' needs (Rose, 1993; Horn, 2010), but Wright (2012) is one of the few researchers to have examined the evidence of what this entailed. Drawing on elementary school logbooks from 1890 to 1918 she showed how head teachers perceived the homes and communities in which their pupils lived:

> The poverty or affluence of the area in which the school was located appears to have been a key defining factor in teachers' attitudes towards pupils and their families and communities. Teachers in schools in poor areas paid more attention in logbooks to families and communities than their counterparts in wealthier areas and were more likely to define and describe these families and communities as a negative influence on pupils. (Wright, 2012, p 160)

There were occasions where head teachers took situations into their own hands to speak to parents about neglect, but they also referred the most serious cases to the National Society for the Prevention of Cruelty to Children (NSPCC), initially founded in 1884. The logbooks showed that teachers in some of the poorest areas of the cities that Wright studied were confronted by cases that would today be defined as 'child protection', while they faced the same challenges that schools still report in coping with staff shortages and absences.

In 1908 the Children Act enshrined in law the concept of 'childhood', which was then extended to the age of 14, although compulsory education was not increased to that age until 1918 (Education Act 1918). Unemployment was high through the 1920s and 1930s and it was estimated that after the Great Depression nearly half of all children suffered from malnutrition and one out of every five children who survived infancy died before they reached 15 (Office of Health Economics, 1962). There were charities such as the NSPCC and Barnardo's, but social services provision was uneven and under-resourced (Jennings, 1947). It is at this point that the Children and Young Persons Act 1933 gave local education departments a more significant role. They became responsible for bringing children in need of care and protection to the court and were pivotal when a court made a 'fit person order', removing a child from home in order to ensure their adequate care or protection. Although two other departments had responsibility for children – the Public Assistance Committee in relation to children voluntarily admitted to care, and Public Health for children covered by various public health Acts – the 1933 Act specified that a local authority should discharge these responsibilities through its education committee.

Improved public health services and better medical and social conditions did lead to fewer children dying throughout the 1930s, but the evacuation of children during World War 2 raised concerns about poverty and ill-health that had largely been ignored in the 1930s. In an examination of the importance of the *Our Towns Report*, produced by the Women's Group on Public Welfare in March 1943, Welshman (1999) describes how wartime exposed high levels of poverty and disease among inner city children, which contributed to the 'mood' for social reform. *The Economist* (1943), for example, had the headline 'Spotlight on poverty', and it argued that evacuation had revealed to the general population 'the black spots in its social life', and *The Lancet* (1943) believed evacuation 'not only provided a large-scale social experiment, but lifted the lid off the less exposed corners of our towns'. It also led to the labelling of the families of such children as 'problem families', a trend still identifiable today. While Welshman (1999) does not attribute the changes that happened during the 1940s to the consequences of the war, the planning that took place during it and a greater consensus on social welfare matters led to a radical revision of the state's role in supporting its population and a shift in favour of 'mild' collectivism as opposed to liberal individualism.

Amid the raft of legislation that emerged between the Education Act 1944 and the Housing Act 1949 was the Children Act 1948. This was the result of a review of services for children that took place towards the end of World War 2 and the framework set out in the report of the Care of Children Committee (1946), usually known as the Curtis Report. The inquiry into the death of Dennis O'Neill had focused attention on the need for reform. He was a 12-year-old boy in the care of Newport Borough Council who had been placed with foster parents in Shropshire where beatings by the foster father caused such extensive injuries that he died. Failures to act on warning signs, poor supervision and a lack of communication between professionals were all identified in a report by Sir William Monckton (Home Office, 1945). As a result, the 1948 Children Act dealt with children in out-of-home care, despite arguments for attention to be given to preventing more children from coming into care (Grover, 2020). Before the Children Act 1948, responsibility for children's welfare was spread across three government ministries – Health, Education and the Home Office – but with the 1948 Act the Home Office was made responsible for the management and oversight of the newly established children's departments in England and Wales. However, abuse or cruelty was not a focus of attention; there are few records about its prevalence because it was not monitored by government. The expectation was that professionals would use their discretion to act if they identified failures in family functioning.

Drawing schools into a multi-agency approach to child protection

In 1967 a report from the Central Advisory Council for Education on primary schools (commonly known as the 'Plowden Report') had referenced the importance of agencies working together for the benefit of children. This point was to be overshadowed by its emphasis on curriculum freedom, which the report's authors believed teachers should have. A year after the Plowden Report, the Seebohm Report (1968) led to the establishment of single social services departments and the generic social work professional and envisaged that these new departments would play a coordinating role across services to meet the needs of families. But both reports had made radical recommendations. The Plowden Report suggested introducing a school social work service to work alongside teachers, and the Seebohm Committee recommended the integration of social work and educational welfare services to provide a family service. The former recommendation was never adopted and very few local authorities implemented the Seebohm vision. According to Parton (2009) it was this vision that informed the *Every Child Matters* reform programme (HM Government, 2003) nearly 40 years later, where the prevention, early intervention and 'think family' themes can be seen as fitting with the original aims of the Seebohm Report. On the other hand, the division of the social work profession between children and adult services, a key part of the ECM reforms, was contrary to the spirit of Seebohm and, it can be argued, has challenged the ability of local authorities to provide effective family services.

It is possible that, with time, recommendations from both the Plowden and Seebohm reports may have found favour but before that could happen local authorities were cast into the spotlight by the report of the inquiry into the death of Maria Colwell at the hands of her stepfather (Department of Health and Social Security, 1974a). According to evidence given to the Jersey Independent Care Inquiry (2014) by Roger Bullock and Roy Parker (see Appendix 6 of the Inquiry report) the concept of child protection as we understand it today was not really on most professionals' horizon before the case of Maria Colwell in 1974 because 'knowledge was scant and a general rule of optimism prevailed' (pp 18–19). But this case catapulted many professions into the child protection arena. The Inquiry report contained criticism of the lack of coordination between different health and welfare agencies and identified the failure of staff in East Sussex County Council, Brighton Council, the NSPCC and the police to work together in effective ways that may have prevented Maria's death. It also identified the failure of schools to share information with each other and with other agencies, and the failure of other agencies to share information with them. The social worker involved in the case had not understood how schools worked. The inquiry recommended establishing formal inter-agency systems for dealing with child abuse, leading to the establishment of area review committees (ARCs), inter-agency child protection conferences to consider specific cases, and child protection registers. A *Memorandum on Non-Accidental Injury to Children* (Department of Health and Social Security, 1974b) was issued to Area Health Authorities and Directors of Social Services and copied to the schools' section of the Department of Education and Science. The memorandum recommended that the Director of Education should be one of the local authority representatives on ARCs.

A series of statutory guidance documents was produced during the 1970s and into the 1980s that described the signs of 'non-accidental injury' (subsequently interpreted as child abuse) in children and the importance of agencies sharing information. Separately, the government's Central Policy Review Staff (1975) had also concluded that political, administrative and professional factors stood in the way of the development of a coordinated network of welfare policies and services and optimistically thought that improved coordination could also lead to cost saving. Thus, it was during this period that both multi-agency operational work as well as multi-agency strategic engagement came to underpin child protection and other policies relating to children's welfare in a more overt way. However, it is important to appreciate that the notion of adopting a joined-up approach to families was in its infancy and, for the most part, schools were on the outside. But it did not have to have been like this.

Education welfare services

It is worth pausing here to consider the role of the EWO. As observed earlier, the forerunners of EWOs were introduced with compulsory education in the 1880s to make sure children attended school. Unlike many mainland European countries and the US, where social workers or school counsellors have been employed by schools for many decades (Sosa et al, 2016), it has been unusual for English schools to do so. However, a national review of the Education Welfare Service, the Ralphs Report (Local Government Training Board, 1974), considered the most appropriate training for EWOs was social work, with the training adapted to take account of the setting where they would be working. Some local authorities paid for EWOs to undergo social work training courses, some insisted on a social work qualification, and, for a short period of time, a few social work courses had a dedicated EWO pathway. In the years that followed there was a battle for control of the service. The Association of Directors of Social Services (ADSS, 1978) argued that the educational welfare service should be located within their departments rather than in schools, where, the Association said, it would be regarded by head teachers as 'relatively insignificant' (p 6) and where EWOs would not have the opportunity for appropriate professional development. On the other hand, the Society of Education Officers (SEO) wanted their service to be based in education and, perhaps referring to the outcome of the Maria Colwell Inquiry and other cases, stated that the:

> indifferent record of social services departments ... does not inspire confidence that an integrated social services approach would be any better ... the common feeling among head teachers is that, in their experience, even the least efficient education welfare officer is likely to be more effectively helpful than a social worker. (SEO, 1979, p 8)

The SEO argument prevailed. The result was that the education welfare services were not joined up with other services that supported families and neither did they have one practice model nor a clear professional identity. The service continued to be both an enforcer of attendance and supporter of welfare.

Schools not at the table

Hallett and Stevenson (1980) viewed the establishment of ARCs as shifting the discourse around concerns about 'problem families' into a focus on the protection of children and identifying families 'at risk'. The same authors conducted a small research study by observing 13 case conferences held in three ARCs. They noted that, along with general practitioners (GPs), teachers were missing from these conferences. Perhaps not surprisingly they found that the conferences were dominated by social services and by their professional jargon, which intimidated others attending. This did not mean that schools did not intervene in relation to children's welfare, but there were few structures to bring them into the 'welfare' tent. The structures that did exist were school based, consisting of welfare duties attached to a class teacher in a primary school or to a form teacher in a secondary school, supplemented by a pastoral system that developed the roles of heads of years or heads of houses by adding responsibility for the welfare of pupils. There was nothing that provided effective links with external professionals such as EWOs, educational psychologists and school nurses. Without a framework, relationships depended on individuals and their willingness to engage with one another.

The Beckford Inquiry

There were also several influential reports into the death of children caused by members of their family or household in this period, which again stressed the importance of professionals working together. One of the most significant was the report produced into the death of Jasmine Beckford, who was killed by her stepfather (London Borough of Brent, 1985). As far as multi-agency work was concerned, the main problem was identified as poor communication between community health and social services, but there had also been communication problems with, and by, her nursery school. The school was not aware that Jasmine was subject of a care order nor that she had been on the Non-Accidental Injuries Register. Her teacher said that if she had known she would have reported bruises on Jasmine's face that her mother said were the result of a fall from a bicycle. Jasmine's non-attendance also went unreported by the school. The Inquiry report commented on the ignorance of child abuse and child care law among the workers centrally involved with Jasmine. Among the many recommendations made in the report was one that in every school a single member of staff should be designated as the liaison officer with the local social services department in respect of every child in care. But at around this time Creighton (1987) examined data collected by the NSPCC from child abuse registers between 1977 and 1984 and found that in 35 per cent of cases where information was available the abuse had come to light through schools. This only served to highlight the inconsistencies that existed in the responses made by schools and probably their awareness of the problems and their complexities.

Preparing teachers for a role in protecting children

Up to this time, and even subsequently, very few publications have focused on schools and child protection. One by Braun (1988) was on the importance of training teachers about child abuse. While it was described as a practical guide and contained a series of exercises, it failed to make any recommendation about the background, experience and skills of anyone delivering the training. Webster (1991) conducted a few small surveys specifically on teachers' understanding of child sexual abuse and concluded that relevant training was not in place. Another book (Maher, 1987), edited by a principal of a community school who was also on the executive of the National Association of Pastoral Care in Education, contains two chapters written by the editor on a school's role in responding to and reducing child abuse, but there was no other contribution from a member of a pastoral team or from a form teacher. However, the proceedings of a seminar on child abuse that had been held in 1986, a year before the book was published, were reported in an appendix. Among the many professionals attending were seven teachers. In the discussions that followed, some of the issues that schools still find challenging were raised. These included relationships with parents if a referral were to be necessary, trust in the way a referral would be handled, and communications within schools and with other agencies. It became clear that there was a lack of understanding among the professionals who attended about the role and responsibilities of one another. Maher (1987) argued that not only did teachers underestimate their significance in this arena, but other professionals also underestimated it. He also identified a lack of knowledge about child abuse among teachers and offered a model that was prescient of that put in place years later, that is a three-level model embracing training for all teachers, additional training for senior managers on their legal responsibilities, and more detailed multi-agency training for those with designated responsibilities.

Although the teachers attending that seminar described procedures for identifying and handling abuse, their interest in child protection was probably atypical of teachers at this time. In preparing this chapter we contacted 12 teachers who we knew from personal contacts had completed their initial training during the 1970s and 1980s and invited them to share their recollections with us. None of the teachers could remember being told when they started working in a school whom they should approach if they had concerns about a child, although they said they found this out as time went on: "I think in our school it was generally common knowledge that the person you would go to if you had any issues would be the senior mistress. There was the old-fashioned senior mistress that looked after that sort of thing. ... Not sure what she did with it" (teacher working in a secondary school in 1980s).

Those who had been senior leaders in schools in this period remembered attending case conferences that were driven by social services and where professional terms were used that they did not understand, echoing the findings of Hallett and Stevenson (1980). They left these meetings thinking that schools were being asked to contribute information rather than to work in partnership. They also remembered 'playing detective' when information was not shared. So, for example, a participant who was a head teacher in this period was shocked to find out that foster parents were not given any background on the children they were looking after:

> 'They would turn up at school with a child and we would not be told in advance. Foster families were not told why the child was taken out of a family home and so could not answer when we asked. Schools would try to find a social worker who could explain what was happening – and then some would, and some wouldn't.' (Head teacher, primary school in 1980s)

We also re-contacted social workers we had spoken with during our research to ask them about their recollections of working with schools in the 1980s. They acknowledged that things had not always worked well and that too much had depended on individuals and local relationships. The most positive accounts came from those who had worked on a 'patch' or locality and had been able to build relationships in their communities, including with schools. Perhaps not surprisingly, it was said to be easier with primary schools than secondary schools because it was easier 'to pop in'. 'Patches' had emerged in some areas of England as a result of the decentralisation measures proposed by the Seebohm Report (Committee on Local Authority and Allied Personal Social Services, 1968) and later by the Barclay Report (Barclay, 1982). They largely disappeared during the late 1980s, when local authorities gradually abandoned the vision of a generalist social work practice and introduced specialised and more centralised services.

The Children Act 1989

It is very difficult to paint a national picture of developments in the 1970s and 1980s because there is very little contemporaneous research to draw upon. Moreover, the recollections that have been considered reflect the two very different worlds of social work and schools, with the occasional bridges created by local practice and by individuals. However, things began to change under the framework that was developed around the Children Act 1989. The recommendations from the Beckford Inquiry, alongside other child abuse inquiries, informed the White Paper (Department of Health and Social Security, 1987) that preceded the drafting of the Children Act 1989. These included the inquiry into the of death of Lester Chapman in 1978 (Hall, 1979), which recommended that each local authority appoint a specialist training officer to help a range of professionals, including teachers, to identify abuse.

But before the Children Act 1989 passed into law the first *Working Together* guidance appeared in which teachers and other school staff were recognised as 'particularly well placed to observe outward signs of abuse, changes in behaviour or failure to develop' (Department of Health and Social Security, 1988, para 4.1). Parton (1991, pp 123–4) identifies this as 'the first time that teachers were officially identified as having a significant role'. The Department for Education and Science (DES) responded by producing Circular 4/88 (Department for Education and Science, 1988) which recommended that 'a senior member of the school's staff should have responsibility, under the procedures established by the LEA [local education authority] for coordinating action within school and for liaison with other agencies'. It also recommended putting in place arrangements for in-service training and, coming so soon after the Cleveland inquiry (Butler-Sloss, 1988), which had discredited a medical procedure that had led to large numbers of children being categorised as having been sexually abused, specifically recognised the need for training in relation to child sexual abuse. However, there was no provision for funding to support these recommendations. In fact, paragraphs 27 and 30 of Circular 4/88 made it clear that additional costs should not be incurred and that arrangements should not have 'significant additional finance or manpower consequences'.

In a House of Lords debate on the then Children Bill, the legislation was described by Lord MacKay, the then Lord Chancellor, as 'the most comprehensive and far-reaching reform of Child Law which has come before Parliament in living memory' (Hansard, 1988). It brought together private and public law affecting children into one place, bringing care and supervision orders under court control, and with it introduced the paramountcy principle into public law, that is that the child's welfare is the court's paramount consideration. It established a balance between statutory powers and responsibilities to keep children safe and children's and parents' rights. A threshold criterion based on the concept of 'significant harm' was introduced as was the definition of children 'in need' of support, with local authorities given responsibility to provide this support to families.

The *Working Together* document that accompanied the Children Act 1989 (Home Office et al, 1991) recognised the key role of schools in protecting children from abuse. However, a survey conducted in 1991 of the main professionals involved in child protection – social workers, health visitors, teachers, police, GPs and paediatricians – found that teachers, along with GPs, had limited involvement in the system and very little understanding or knowledge of that system (Hallett and Birchall, 1992). The survey had been conducted just at the point when schools were becoming more aware of their responsibilities but not necessarily confident of how to fulfil them. The Audit Commission (1994) noted that, while health, education and social services shared a common concern for the well-being of children, in only a very small number of local authorities had effective inter-agency working been developed. One way to achieve this was through training.

Training and support for teachers

During the 1990s training and support for schools increased, as did the willingness of schools to assume these responsibilities, evidenced by a series of surveys of local education authorities (LEAs), schools and institutions providing Initial Teacher Training (ITTs) conducted in 1997 (reported in Baginsky, 2000). A survey of LEAs in England found that they were all offering a consultation service of some sort on child protection to their schools, which was often available to independent (private fee-paying) schools as well. Ninety per cent of responders were also providing training, often in collaboration with the then social services departments. In 1995/1996 and 1997/1998 LEAs had been able to apply for funding to support training as, in both years, child protection was one of the specified headings under the Department for Education and Employment (DfEE) Grants for Education Support and Training (GEST). The vast majority had made at least one bid and this additional support played a key part in boosting the number of designated teachers who were trained. All but one of the 327 schools replying to the school survey conducted by Baginsky (2000), which had an 85 per cent response rate, had a designated teacher who had accessed training and had a child protection policy in place. In two thirds of these schools all teachers had had at least some training. So, even if it had taken some time to achieve, over a reasonably short period of time, since the Children Act 1989 and the 1991 *Working Together* document, significant progress had been made. Most of these schools were also trying to attend child protection conferences whenever possible, although concerns emerged over the difficulties encountered in communicating with social services and the delays around making and receiving information about referrals.

The survey of ITTs was sent to conveners of teacher training courses, both those in higher education institutions (HEIs) and the then new School Centred Initial Teacher Training (SCITT) courses; 82 per cent of all ITT courses and half of the 28 SCITTs responded. However, the responses from both were similar. The majority did something but not very much and it appeared to be bolted on rather than integrated. In the case of HEIs, it was usually bolted on after the first school-based placement or even after the last placement.

An important subsequent development was the distribution of Circular 4/98 *Teaching: High Status, High Standards* (Department for Education and Employment, 1998). This set out requirements for all ITT courses by including one standard in the newly introduced ITT curriculum: 'for all courses, those to be awarded Qualified Teacher Status, when assessed, demonstrate that they have a working knowledge and understanding of teachers' liabilities and responsibilities' (p 16).

The Labour government's (1997–2010) reforms

On coming to power in 1997, Tony Blair, the Prime Minister of the first Labour-led government for 18 years, had announced that his priority was 'education, education, education', a commitment he had first made at the Labour Party Conference in 1996 (Purcell, 2020). The White Paper *Excellence in Schools* referred to the 'unrelenting pressure on schools and teachers for improvement' (Department for Education and Employment, 1997, p 11) and the School Standards and Framework Act 1998 was intended to support the development of a 'World Class' education service. During the first of three Labour terms of government, between 1997 and 2001, the main priority was to raise standards of achievement, measured through children's and schools' performance in statutory examinations at the 'key stages' of education. Education reforms introduced in this period did emphasise the welfare role of schools in so far as schools were expected to promote the 'social inclusion' of children, but this was generally framed as a key contributor to the goal of raising standards.

Soon after coming to power the Social Exclusion Unit was established by the Labour government to coordinate policymaking on specified cross-cutting topics, one of which was truancy. One of its reports (Social Exclusion Unit, 1998) led to a government commitment to achieve a one-third reduction in truancy levels by 2002. LEAs were made responsible for ensuring that children attended school regularly, a role carried out by the educational welfare service. Despite calls for the service to be overhauled and for the potential contribution it could make to children's welfare to be recognised (Halford, 1994; Pritchard et al, 1998), this did not happen. In most places EWOs were based in LEAs and not well integrated into schools, and, as described earlier, LEAs were also facing their own problems. In its evidence to a House of Commons Children's Schools and Families Select Committee (2009) the National Association of Social Workers in Education reported research it had commissioned which found that in a sample of EWOs just over a quarter held a social work qualification, with 18 per cent having no qualifications at all. Despite this, an audit of EWOs' work in four local authorities had shown that, among those pupils they were working with over truancy and other attendance problems, many had serious and complex needs that did not trigger the threshold for social worker support (Ryan et al, 2008). The Association wanted to see a specialist role recognised and developed within the structures that existed. Instead, it continued to be what one author had described 30 years previously as the 'Cinderella type of service' (Robinson, 1978).

As schools were given increasing responsibility for their funding and more control over their own budgets, they began to employ more agencies and individuals whose work overlapped with EWOs, to meet specific needs and circumstances. Reid (2008) listed some of these: 'home-school liaison officers, attendance officers, classroom assistants, learning school mentors, police liaison officers, out-of-school learning support staff, attendance secretaries, first-day absence support staff, regional truancy advisers, social workers and behavioural support staff, among others' (p 175).

The challenge that schools faced in terms of meeting their welfare responsibilities, and the continued importance of working closely with LEAs in this regard, was highlighted by a second survey of LEAs carried out in 2002 (Baginsky, 2003). The feedback received from LEAs on their experience of multi-agency work resonates with experiences recounted nearly 20 years later which are reported here in later chapters. Even those who assessed multi-agency work to be progressing reasonably well thought that its effectiveness was challenged by several factors. They considered the thresholds at which the then social services intervened in relation to 'children in need of protection' and 'children in need' to be far too high. The majority believed either that the system in place was not working as intended or that a system to support all children did not exist.

The Education Act 2002 and the Every Child Matters reforms

By the time that research was completed in 2007 two important events had occurred. Section 175 of the Education Act 2002 had placed a duty on LEAs, maintained (state) schools and further education institutions (often educating young people aged 16 and over) to exercise their functions with a view to safeguarding and promoting the welfare of children, and section 157 placed the same duty on independent schools, including academies. The second, and not unrelated event, was a significant shift in policy which had yet to be reflected in practice. It had started with the White Paper, *Schools Achieving Success* (Department for Education and Skills, 2001), which noted that the government's Children's Fund would provide extra money for preventative work with vulnerable children and young people. The shift accelerated after a report by the Joint Chief Inspectors (Department of Health, 2002) found that, while all agencies accepted their responsibility to ensure that children were safeguarded, this was not always reflected in practice. This followed the findings of the Laming inquiry (Laming, 2003) into the death of Victoria Climbié. The government's response was contained in the Green Paper *Every Child Matters* (HM Government, 2003) and the *Every Child Matters: Next Steps* document (HM Government, 2004), culminating in the Children Act 2004.

The overriding vision of the ECM policy framework was to strengthen prevention while strengthening protection. The ambition was to improve outcomes for all children – defined in terms of being healthy, staying safe, enjoying and achieving, making a positive contribution and achieving economic well-being – and to narrow the gap between those who did well and those who did not. This required far more agencies and practitioners to be responsible for safeguarding the welfare of children. At the same time the Office for Standards in Education, Children's Services and Skills (Ofsted) began to inspect schools in England in relation to the effectiveness of their safeguarding arrangements and to judge them on how they were meeting their statutory responsibilities. Over the years the intensity with which this is done has increased and, at the time when the research reported in this book was conducted, a school was judged to be inadequate if its policy and procedures on safeguarding were found to be ineffective (Ofsted, 2015a).[1]

Back in 2004, if outcomes for children were to be improved, as envisaged by ECM, then all relevant agencies would need to be part of a reshaped model of service delivery. The programme assumed that education, social services and health services would secure some level of integration with the development of the proposed Children's Trusts. Bringing together joint commissioning and joint delivery, these Trusts would be at the heart of the policy agenda, which necessitated that 'all existing structures and practices were reviewed and revised' (Leadbetter, 2008, p 198). Meanwhile some local authorities had begun to amalgamate their education and children's social services departments. Every local authority had to appoint a children's director to be accountable for children's services, including education and children's social care, and a lead councillor to hold political responsibility for child welfare and to be accountable for outcomes for children in their area. It was at this point that LSCBs were created. At the operational level three new initiatives were designed to facilitate closer inter-agency working.

Box 2.1: Initiatives to facilitate closer inter-agency working

Common Assessment Framework (CAF): A framework to help practitioners work with children, young people and families to assess children and young people's additional needs for earlier and more effective services, develop a common understanding of those needs and how to work together to meet them.

Team Around the Child (TAC): Where a multi-agency response is required, the formation of a TAC brings together practitioners from across different services who work together to coordinate and deliver an integrated package of solution-focused support to meet the needs identified during the common assessment framework.

Lead professional: The person responsible for coordinating the actions identified in the assessment process; a single point of contact for children and young people with additional needs, supported by more than one practitioner within a TAC.

Source: Children's Workforce Development Council, 2009

While schools had little option but to engage at some level, the extent to which they did depended in part on the support and training that were available, as well as the cultures in agencies and professions that were receptive to multi-agency working (Baginsky, 2007).

In a survey conducted for *The Guardian* newspaper in 2009 of social workers in children's services, 72 per cent believed ECM had improved the quality of care for children and 74 per cent said it had improved joint working with other professionals (Brindle, 2009). So, it is unfortunate that, while never formally abandoned, it was sidelined when the Coalition Government came to power after the 2010 election. One of its first actions was to rename the Department for Children, Schools and Families (DCSF) the Department for Education (DfE), and the ECM logo – a brightly coloured rainbow – which stretched across the atrium in the Department's building was torn down. An internal DfE memo contained two columns, one for words not to be used after 11 May (when the Coalition took office) and one for those that replaced them. These included the term 'help children achieve more' in place of ECM's five outcomes (Puffett, 2010).

Welfare professionals based in schools

It is also important to reflect briefly on experiences of welfare professionals who have been based in schools. In this final section evaluations of two programmes involving the placement of two groups of welfare professionals initiated under the Labour government are briefly considered.

Social workers in schools: Several of the social work remodelling pilot initiatives supported by the DCSF between 2009 and 2011 (Baginsky et al, 2011) were based in or closely linked with schools. The pilot projects were developed to allow local authorities to explore different ways of delivering social work practice and they were provided with additional resources to address the deficits they identified in providing effective social work to children and their families. There were 11 pilots altogether and several focused on supporting schools, including the one developed by the City of Westminster. Here the intention was to integrate social workers within schools, where they would provide a consultative role as well as carrying out early intervention and providing advice on statutory work arising from these settings. This proved much easier to achieve in primary schools which already had a strong commitment to ensuring that all school staff had responsibility for supporting families and safeguarding children. Head teachers and staff believed that this role was enhanced by the presence of a social worker. One head teacher, who had been in post for over 20 years, declared she had 'waited all my professional life for something like this' (Baginsky et al, 2011, p 58). The social workers provided advice and support to parents and worked to improve understanding of thresholds and appropriate referrals. However, in the Westminster secondary school there was an expectation that the presence of a social worker would take pressure off staff by dealing with all actual and potential child protection problems that arose and be a direct link into statutory services. This contrasted with the real intention, which was to facilitate engagement of the school with a range of professionals and work alongside them. The school expected to hold the social worker to account by providing feedback on the progress of cases already being handled by children's social care and explaining what had happened if other social workers had failed to make contact. The social worker found the placement difficult. She did not like being away from colleagues and did not feel welcome or well integrated into the school. The tensions around this only served to further undermine the credibility of the role. When she left to take up a post in another authority her replacement was determined to make the boundaries of the role explicit, while at the same time improving the ways in which the school and other agencies communicated. Within a short time, the school had embraced the concept as well as the person in that role. The school staff put this down to this social worker being willing to be part of the school: 'She talks to staff and pupils, and she addresses concerns. She has made herself available and part of the school. She sits in the inclusion office. She has picked up difficult cases – ones which probably needed social workers, but which would not have met the threshold' (Baginsky et al, 2011, p 60). As with so many initiatives, these pilots did not survive when the funding ended but it would have been interesting to have had the opportunity to assess the impact of this support on future relationships and practice as well as children's outcomes.

Counsellors in schools: The second example involved placing counselling teams in schools. In 2016 over a third (36 per cent) of schools in England provided school-based support for students' emotional and mental well-being but by 2019 research by Place2Be and the National Association of Head Teachers found this had almost doubled to 66 per cent (Place2Be, 2020). It is surprising, therefore, that there has been very little research conducted on this subject and that that which has been undertaken has usually set out to assess impact. However, one study explored both the impact of a counselling service and how it became embedded in schools (Baginsky, 2005). The NSPCC established 14 school teams across England, Wales and Northern Ireland to work in primary and secondary schools. These teams were led by social workers, some of whom held a counselling qualification, but all team members were qualified counsellors. The concept brought together three professions – teachers, social workers and counsellors. Many teachers in the schools admitted that their ability to respond to the needs of children had been severely constrained by the demands imposed on them to reach various targets so they were very happy to welcome the teams, but this did not avert difficulties that emerged when different professional cultures were brought together. Insufficient attention was paid to ensuring that most teachers understood the principles of counselling or social work or that counsellors and social workers understood schools and the educational context into which they had moved. So, while counsellors in schools stood apart, not going into the staffroom or having any social contact with teachers, seeing this as linked to the professional distance required, from the schools' perspective they were seen to be aloof. There were also differences in the philosophies of counselling and social work, particularly social work practices in a child protection agency. In most of the teams the counsellors accepted the ground rules of working for a child protection agency and that a strict code of confidentiality would have to be negotiated. But there was one team where the counsellors refused to accept this, and the situation became one where positions became entrenched and the team untenable. The school team manager, employed by a child protection agency, admitted that she was in the position of not knowing who the team members were talking to in schools or what they were talking about:

> Their expectation of counselling supervision was that they bring stuff that they want to talk about. We are a child protection agency, and it is not possible to accommodate those expectations, particularly as they are not child protection trained. The agency wants to know what clients say and what is being said to clients because maybe they are not picking up on things. (School team manager quoted in Baginsky, 2005, p 120)

Both these examples of welfare professionals working in schools shine a light on the difficulties that can arise when different professional cultures come together but also on how these cultures may be more firmly embedded in individuals than in the professions. While there were difficulties in elements of both, there was also practice that could have been used to steer future engagement if the innovations had continued.

Reflections on the development of the role of schools in child protection and safeguarding

Susannah Wright, Senior Lecturer in Education Studies, School of Education, Oxford Brookes University

It is important to take a long view. Maybe I would say that, coming to this as a historian. I would dispute any simple learning of lessons from the past, or of lifting policies and frameworks from one period and context and dropping them in another. Nonetheless, some insights into a more distant past help us to understand the recent past and the present: this chapter at the outset intended to 'understand a little of the journey' towards the role that schools are now playing in multi-agency approaches to child protection and safeguarding. For me, this chapter helps to elucidate why certain possibilities are open while others are closed, why we have the language and framings that we do, a complex and overlapping network of concepts around child welfare, child protection and child safeguarding.

The journey described in Chapter 2 has not been uniform or perhaps even uni-directional. As noted early in the chapter, interest in child welfare has ebbed and flowed. Drawing on wider scholarship, however, a pattern emerges of schools, and the people in them, becoming locations in which welfare and child protection become visible, and are tackled by teachers and other school employees, sometimes with referral to a range of voluntary and state agencies (or the individuals who represent them in the locality). In my own research (Wright 2009; 2012) I looked up close through local case studies of urban areas in the late 19th and early 20th centuries at the nature of these interactions in and around schools. Others discussed in this chapter have taken a broader sweep, eliciting a national picture. A more detailed discussion of recent decades reveals a complex picture of policy and practice.

Quite rightly, legislation and national policy feature as a key framework – these after all helped to create the categories of workers and to shape their practice. Indeed, a core dynamic that emerges through this chapter is the intersection of this policy landscape, the national and the local, and the people working within it who enact policy, but also shape it through their actions towards the children and other adults they work with while pursuing child welfare and child protection goals. A further important strand concerns the role of the media and public debate. This is credited in this chapter for creating a focus on child protection and preventing harm from the 1970s onwards. The focus on individual children in media debates of more recent decades is, perhaps, a contrast with much earlier moral panics surrounding a generic and stigmatising category of the 'slum child'. Teachers, the NSPCC and others, of course, dealt with individuals, but individuals were less central to public and media debate.

Schools and their employees have, since the mid 19th-century period that this chapter started with, worked for child welfare and child protection, and worked with other agencies and individuals outside the school. These processes have not been smooth or even, but the work of schools in this area has been significant since the early years of mass education and will continue to be so.

3

Contemporary challenges: views
from local authorities and 'the field'

Introduction

The purpose of the early phases of our research was to build a picture of the contemporary challenges facing those with a responsibility for the safeguarding and protection of school age children. As explained in Chapter 1, this began with a literature review and interviews with 68 professionals working in children's social care or education services in England and an additional 26 interviews with people working in regional and national agencies involved in different aspects of safeguarding and education policy. These interviews, which took place in the spring and summer of 2017, informed our subsequent national surveys of local authority education safeguarding leads, children's social care leads and LSCB managers. Building a more up-to-date picture in this way was essential in developing our understanding of how schools and other agencies were responding to the perennial concerns identified in our historical analysis and the earlier study (Baginsky, 2007), as well as identifying the new challenges with which they were currently grappling. The purpose of this chapter is to summarise the key findings of this preliminary work, drawing on our literature review, interviews with those working in the field, and the surveys.

Inevitably the findings discussed in this chapter reflect the perspectives of those working in local authorities, either in children's social care or those with responsibility for safeguarding in education, as well as those in agencies with a broader remit but whose work impacts on, or brings them into contact with, schools. The important point is that they are not normally working within or employed by schools, which contrasts with the findings reported in the remaining chapters of this book, which provide a view from the inside, drawing on our extensive interviews with staff working in schools.

This chapter begins with a discussion of the changing relationship between schools and local authorities in the context of academisation and austerity. The second section examines the support provided to schools by local authorities and partner agencies. In the third section the ever-widening scope of safeguarding work and the responsibilities placed on schools are considered, focusing on the specific examples of online safety, the sexual and criminal exploitation of children, and the UK's national Prevent strategy, designed to combat terrorism. The next two sections consider the development of policies and processes around cases that schools refer to children's social care and cases below the children's social care threshold but where an 'early help' intervention may be necessary. Anne Edwards shares her thoughts on the findings presented in this chapter in the final section.

Academisation, austerity and the role of local authorities

The initial impetus for our research was to examine how schools and other local agencies were responding to the potential tensions created between academisation, a policy that promoted greater school autonomy, and safeguarding duties, which, by both their nature and statute, require integrated multi-agency working. However, in our initial discussions with local authorities and others working in the field, it quickly became apparent that it was extremely difficult, if not impossible, to separate the impact of academisation from funding cuts to local government and the wider public sector following nearly a decade of austerity. As more and more schools have become academies, and consequently receive their funding directly from central government, the resources available to local authorities have significantly diminished. But the impact of this trend has been compounded by the effect of austerity and the year-on-year cuts to centrally allocated funding for local authorities. Moreover, as we noted in Chapter 1, these funding cuts were more severe for local authorities serving the poorest communities, where central government grants have historically made up a greater proportion of their income than has council tax (local taxation) (Webb and Bywaters, 2018).

In response to cuts in funding, either because of academisation or austerity, many local authorities were forced to close or reconfigure services which schools previously relied upon such as education welfare, behaviour support and family support services. As one school improvement adviser explained,

'There has been a strangulation of local authority support for schools in these areas. My role is purely to hold schools to account for standards – the support we give is in relation to teaching, learning, assessment and leadership. Before – say 10 or 15 years ago – we had a well-funded specialist support team that worked with schools in a joined-up way – things like behaviour and support teams and outreach – they have gone as there is no budget to do those things.' (School improvement advisor, metropolitan borough)

The loss of these welfare support services not only reduced the support available to schools, but it also limited the capacity of local authorities to monitor and influence welfare practices within schools. When a referral is made to children's social care in relation to a school-aged child their school attendance is one of the first checks made as this is considered to be a key protective factor in safeguarding children and young people (Rasasingham, 2015; Oldfield et al, 2016). As a direct consequence of academisation, local authorities no longer have automatic access to all schools' attendance and exclusions data. While only one local authority reported any difficulties in obtaining this information and from one academy chain, many of those we spoke to in local authorities felt that something had been lost by not having direct access to data on attendance and exclusions. This introduced delays and made it difficult to check the accuracy of reporting on attendance or the appropriateness of exclusions for pupils if there were wider welfare concerns.

Furthermore, over recent years concerns have been raised by national agencies regarding the number of 'invisible children' (Children's Commissioner, 2019) who do not attend school and where local authorities lack the capacity and legal authority to ensure that their educational and safeguarding needs are being met. Officially, many of these children are deemed to be 'home educated', an arrangement which can work perfectly well for some (Davies, 2015). However, this number has grown steadily over recent years. The Association of Directors of Children's Services (ADCS) estimated that over 86,000 children spent at least some time in home education during the 2019/20 academic year[1] (ADCS, 2020). This is concerning because for many children and families this was not an arrangement that had been entered into willingly or that was in the best interests of the child or young person. In some instances, parents may decide to remove their child from school because they do not feel that they 'fit in' to a particular school environment (Children's Commissioner, 2019). But more alarmingly, there is evidence to suggest that some schools are pressuring parents to remove their child from school, a practice often referred to as 'off-rolling' (Children's Commissioner, 2019). The ADCS (2019) highlighted specific concerns among local authorities relating to the growing number of Key Stage 4 pupils (aged 14 to 16) being pressured to move to home education as General Certificate of Secondary Education (GCSE) examinations approach. Equally worrying were examples of parents thought to have removed their children from school to take advantage of the light touch regulation and 'keep out of sight' of children's social care services (Children's Commissioner, 2019). Moreover, some parents claiming to be educating their children at home are sending them to unregistered and illegal schools considered by the Children's Commissioner (2019) to offer 'a substandard education' and where 'welfare standards are dubious' (p 14).

Responding to these concerns, in 2018 the DfE initiated a consultation and call for evidence to seek views on the creation of local authority registers of children not attending school and duties on parents and the proprietors of certain education settings (DfE, 2018b). However, at the time of writing (end of 2021) the DfE had yet to publish the findings of this exercise. We found that the concerns raised at the national level were strongly reflected in the views of the local authority education officers we interviewed and those who responded to questions in our national surveys on this topic. The biggest challenge local authorities reported was maintaining up-to-date information about children living in the local area but who were not attending school. As a result, there was strong support not only for the creation of local registers, but also for national agencies including what are now (in 2021) the UK Visas and Immigration Agency, Her Majesty's Revenue and Customs, the NHS, and the Department of Work and Pensions to play a stronger role in supporting local authorities to track the movement of children and families. They also supported the imposition of new duties on parents and education providers; more action to stem the practice of off-rolling; and stronger powers for local authorities to be able to visit families who are educating children at home. Support for the last point was, however, tempered by concerns regarding the availability of the resources that would be required to do this.

Multi-agency safeguarding arrangements

We noted in Chapter 1 that, during the course of our research, the government announced that LSCBs were to be replaced under new multi-agency safeguarding arrangements (DfE, 2018a). LSCBs were established in 2006 as the accountable body for multi-agency safeguarding in all local areas, bringing together a range of key agencies, including schools. Their demise followed a review by Sir Alan Wood (Wood, 2016), a former teacher and chief executive of the Hackney Learning Trust, who has been described as 'a go-to fixer of children's services departments' (Butler, 2014). Wood's recommendation that LSCBs be scrapped and replaced with new multi-agency arrangements, under which schools would not be one of the three statutory 'safeguarding partners' was accepted by the DfE and incorporated into the Children and Social Work Act 2017. The detail on how the new arrangements would be expected to operate was incorporated into the 2018 version of *Working Together* (DfE, 2018a). All local areas were required to have the new arrangements in place by September 2019.

Thus, at the time of our scoping interviews and national surveys (mid 2017–early 2018) there was uncertainty regarding the transition from LSCBs to the new arrangements and widespread concern regarding the future representation of education services and schools. It was clear from research carried out shortly before Wood's review that LSCBs were maturing and becoming more successful in leading and negotiating multi-agency relationships, but that there were limitations in how far they could compel agencies to act (Baginsky and Holmes, 2015). Moreover, Wood's recommendation to scrap rather than strengthen the ability of LSCBs to hold local organisations to account and encourage them to use the powers of scrutiny that already exist in legislation was questioned (Jones and Blyth, 2016). The subsequent announcement of the details of the new arrangements, but specifically the categorisation of schools as a 'relevant agency' rather than a 'safeguarding partner', also drew widespread criticism from a range of organisations, including the ADCS, the British Association of Social Workers and the National Association of Head Teachers (see O'Connell, 2018; Purcell, 2020).

The rationale for adopting this change can be traced to one statement in his report where Wood (2016) points to the impossibility of representing schools effectively. A survey of LSCBs by Baginsky and Holmes (2015) found that nearly three quarters of chairs of LSCBs thought that the increasing independence of schools had made it harder to engage with them, but they also reported similar concerns about reorganised health services. However, health, represented by NHS Clinical Commissioning Groups, went on to be a statutory partner. Although there was a limit to the number of people who could be on the executive board of LSCBs, a large part of their work took place in sub-groups where LSCBs were seeking creative ways to engage schools and where they were often very well represented. Before they were replaced, LSCBs were working hard to establish different ways of engaging schools and there is a strong argument that they should have been given the chance to prove their effectiveness.

These concerns were reflected in the views of those we interviewed and surveyed. But, more positively, it was apparent that in many areas the aim was to try to maintain and strengthen relationships with schools despite their new 'relevant agency' status. Reflecting on the replacement of LSCBs one participant commented:

> 'The well-documented failure of the Act [Children and Social Work Act 2017] to make education settings a statutory partner is both a missed opportunity and one that carries with it risks. We are still developing our future Safeguarding Partnership arrangements, but on a local level we will continue to try and engage education providers on the same footing as other statutory partners.' (LSCB, unitary authority)

Notwithstanding the difficulties that local authorities faced in the context of academisation policies and reductions in funding, the importance of maintaining positive working relationships with all schools was continuously emphasised by the local authority managers we interviewed. Moreover, it appeared that the quality of these relationships was generally unconnected to whether a school had academy status or not. It appeared that many schools that had initially sought to distance themselves from local authorities after converting to academy status were now increasingly re-engaging as they sought to fulfil their safeguarding responsibilities. As one participant explained:

> 'I think when schools became academies, they felt that they could deal with all the issues that were within their own school and I think there has been a realisation ... that actually they need a relationship back with the local area to deal with some of the complex situations. So, I don't see any barriers now between local authority engagement and academies. We treat all schools the same. ... The message that local authorities weren't helpful to schools I think has now almost disappeared.' (Head of education, unitary authority)

It was also explained that schools saw the importance of making sure that their own safeguarding policies and procedures were consistent with local arrangements. Thus, most schools, including those in large academy chains, had either adapted model policies and procedures recommended by the local authority or at least mapped their own against them.

Safeguarding support for schools

The importance of multi-agency working in relation to safeguarding was reflected in the levels of support and training provided by local authorities and LSCBs at the time of our interviews and surveys. Although funding cuts had greatly affected the availability of services such as family support and education welfare, 89 of the 93 local authorities we surveyed confirmed that they had an education safeguarding service in place. These services were generally located within local authority education departments but worked closely with children's social care and LSCBs. Just under half confirmed that this service was provided at no cost to schools. In other areas the service operated as a traded service, meaning that schools contributed to covering at least some of the operating costs. In areas where schools were required to pay, take-up was nevertheless very high including among academies and independent schools.[2] Some services comprised just one officer whereas in other areas small teams provided dedicated support.

Significantly, three quarters of education and children's social care respondents to our survey confirmed that education safeguarding teams had not been cut back over the previous five years, despite cuts identified earlier to education welfare, family support and behaviour support teams. The continued prioritisation of this dedicated support to schools seemed to be connected to the steady increase in duties placed on schools over recent years, as outlined in Chapter 2. The main tasks carried out by education safeguarding services were aimed at ensuring compliance with these duties and generally included the provision of model safeguarding policies, carrying out school audits, and helping with Ofsted inspection preparation and post-inspection recommendations. Local authority participants believed that these services were also highly valued by schools for the *ad hoc* advice and support they offered, particularly when faced with difficult decisions regarding a specific case or when they were struggling with a referral to children's social care. In some areas education safeguarding leads also facilitated local network meetings and events where schools' DSLs could come together and share best practice ideas and offer mutual support.

Schools also rely on external support to ensure that DSLs and all other staff receive the levels of training they need to meet their safeguarding responsibilities in line with statutory guidance in *Keeping Children Safe in Education* (DfE, 2021a). Understandably, the training requirements for DSLs are more comprehensive than for other staff, usually requiring them to attend several days of external training when they first take up the role and regular refresher courses thereafter. For other teaching and non-teaching staff basic training is generally delivered in school by the head or DSL, very often as part of an in-service training day – all schools have five such days each year. Additionally, schools may also choose to send DSLs or other members of staff on external training relating to specific aspects of safeguarding they are concerned about, or in some cases invite trainers in to deliver additional whole-school training on a topic such as on online safety when it may be felt that all staff need enhanced awareness.

In our research we found that in most areas LSCBs delivered or commissioned training for local DSLs, including those employed by academies and independent schools. LSCBs also offered a range of more specific courses covering a wide range of safeguarding topics which were made available to all schools. Respondents to our LSCB survey believed that the available training closely matched the needs of schools, although they acknowledged that some wanted more training on specific topics such as mental health and internet safety. We also found an even split between those who charged schools for DSL and other training and those that did not, with academies slightly more likely to have to pay compared with maintained schools. Despite this training offer, some local authority education and LSCB managers we interviewed expressed concern about some schools relying on online training modules for whole-staff training. Concerns about the use of independent trainers, including for initial DSL training, were also raised. As one head of school improvement explained:

'When I came here the schools were up in arms because they had been given an exemplar safeguarding policy that was deemed by Ofsted not to be fit for purpose. That is not helpful. We need absolute confidence that people that are doing training for us are at top of their game.' (Head of school improvement, metropolitan borough)

On the other hand, one of the Regional Schools Commissioners offered a more nuanced view regarding the use of independent trainers. In their opinion schools were very conscious of Serious Case Reviews that had pointed to schools failing to take appropriate action to protect children, but which also pointed to wider failings in local systems:

> 'I do know that some multi-academy trusts (MATs), large and small, prefer to get their training from independent specialists, rather than from local authorities, because that, in their view, if they are getting it from the local authority in which they work, they don't completely trust it. There is a bit of an inbuilt tension in there. Certainly, from my experience many trusts do both. So, they take the free training from LSCB, if not directly from LAs [local authorities], probably because they think they would be in a better position if they are seen to have done it, if we are going to be absolutely honest. But they also would then hire specialists to provide additional training.' (Regional school commissioner)

Furthermore, it is important to emphasise that we did not uncover evidence to suggest that schools or academy trusts were completely dismissive of training offered by their local authority or LSCB. Rather, it was apparent that some schools were drawing on as many sources of support as they could, including a mix of local authority/LSCB, trust safeguarding leads and independent trainers to ensure that they had done all they could to prepare staff and put them in a good position to be able to make informed decisions.

The extended scope of safeguarding

It was clear from our interviews and surveys that local authorities continued to regard the provision of support and training to schools, regardless of their status, as very important. Significantly, the development of national safeguarding policies has greatly extended the scope of schools' safeguarding responsibilities, making them more dependent upon external agencies, including local authorities. In this context, it is understandable that schools continued to engage with local authorities and LSCBs despite the political emphasis on school autonomy and the championing of academy trusts ahead of local authorities.

The full extent of schools' responsibilities is set out in the *Keeping Children Safe in Education* guidance (DfE, 2021a), a document which has been regularly updated and added to over recent years. This guidance includes four main sections covering the responsibilities of all staff working in schools; the management of safeguarding; safer recruitment practices; and dealing with allegations or concerns raised in relation to staff, volunteers and contractors.

The guidance stipulates that all staff must be alert to potential indicators of child abuse and neglect and understand how to respond. Previous versions of this guidance had emphasised the importance of understanding the dangers children faced in the family home. However, a series of Serious Cases Reviews and wider policy reviews have highlighted the dangers and risks faced by children and young people in the wider community. Research drawing on the concept of 'contextual safeguarding' (Firmin, 2017) has also emphasised the importance of focusing on what happens to children outside the home, and contextual safeguarding is now referenced in the guidance (DfE, 2021a). Moreover, *Keeping Children Safe in Education* has been updated to incorporate an extended range of specific safeguarding concerns, including online safety, child exploitation (sexual and criminal), female genital mutilation, radicalisation and mental health. Over more recent years there has also been a greater awareness of peer-on-peer sexual abuse *in* schools and following a recent review by Ofsted (2021) this concern featured prominently in the 2021 version of the DfE guidance.

In our interviews and national surveys we asked participants what they thought about schools' preparedness in responding to three specific safeguarding concerns which were high on the policymaking agenda at the time. These were online safety; child exploitation; and preventing radicalisation.

Online safety

The central role of the internet in daily life, facilitated in large part by the explosion in smartphone use over recent years, was not envisaged by any participants in Baginsky's (2007) earlier study. In 2008 just 17 per cent of the UK population owned a smartphone, but this had grown to 78 per cent overall and 95 per cent for 16–24-year-olds when our study began (Ofcom, 2018). This profound change has created major opportunities for those who are connected, but it has also created new dangers, particularly for young people. Concerns regarding the grooming of children and young people by adults online are widely reported in the media and most children's social care managers responding to our survey had observed a moderate or substantial increase in cases where online safety was a concern. The internet also provides young people with easy access to sexually explicit material. In 2019 nearly a third of 12–15-year-olds reported that they had seen online content that they found to be 'worrying' or 'nasty' (NSPCC, 2020). Smartphone and social media use among young people is also connected to peer-on-peer abuse, including online bullying and the sharing of explicit personal pictures or videos. Not surprisingly, it is now considered to be a contributing factor to poor mental health (Ofsted, 2021).

In response, policymakers have consistently looked towards schools to play a major role in protecting children and young people from potentially harmful online material. The use of filtering and monitoring systems on school or college IT systems is an important component of online safety policies. However, given that so many young people can access the internet via mobile networks using their own smartphones, schools must carefully consider how phones are used on their premises and be alert to their inappropriate use, including the sharing of explicit images or videos. Moreover, this is now one of the key safeguarding responsibilities of *all* staff, not just safeguarding leads and senior managers. Broadly, schools need to play a role in educating pupils and staff about staying safe online (DfE, 2021a), but this is a complex area and schools require appropriate support to do so. Many schools are also working closely with parents to educate them about online safety and pick up the pieces from incidents involving pupils outside of school hours. As one education adviser explained, "On a Monday morning those staff responsible for pastoral issues will have a queue of people – children and people – because something has happened over the weekend, in primary and secondary schools and even early years" (Education adviser, unitary authority). Clearly, expectations placed on schools in this area have grown considerably even though their capacity and authority to monitor what happens to their pupils online remain limited. While three fifths of education safeguarding leads we surveyed thought that schools had the confidence to deal with problems relating to online safety, others were more circumspect, including LSCB leads, who were slightly less likely to agree with this. One LSCB respondent commented:

'Often schools refer to the issues of online safety and social media as being chronic in nature, that is long-term and constant with periodic crises that require an enhanced safeguarding response. As a Board, we include online safety issues in every school training briefing we deliver, but we know this is likely not sufficient.' (LSCB, unitary authority)

Concerns regarding schools' practice in this area were also raised in our interviews with local authority managers who had been involved in dealing with incidents involving indecent images. The national expert on internet safety we interviewed was also concerned about schools not always responding to incidents in line with the messages given in training and national guidance:

'We see schools, even those with great policies and those with best intentions often do the wrong things. An example we cite is a technical manager in a secondary school who discovered a sexting image on the network and thought "I need to bring this to the head's attention." He copied it from the student area of the network to the teachers' area and then thought it might get deleted so he printed a copy and sent it to the head. He went on to do more "distribution". He had the best of intentions, but it was completely the wrong thing to do. Recognition, response and resolution is vital. If any device is involved, it should be switched off and reported to [the] DSL – do nothing else. It is for [the] DSL to manage.' (National expert on internet safety)

Furthermore, one education safeguarding adviser felt that the training and support provided by local authorities and LSCBs had become more inconsistent after the closure of the British Educational Communications and Technology Agency (BECTA) following the government's spending review conducted in 2010. BECTA had been the lead agency across the UK for promotion and integration of information and communications technology (ICT) in education and was playing a key coordinating role in this area before it disappeared.

Child sexual exploitation and child criminal exploitation

The inclusion of sexual and criminal exploitation in the *Keeping Children Safe in Education* guidance (DfE, 2021a) has formed part of the government's response to heightened awareness of the dangers facing some children and young people in their local communities. The inclusion of child sexual exploitation (CSE) followed high-profile reports detailing the systematic sexual exploitation of teenage girls by gangs of men in Rotherham (Jay, 2014) and Oxfordshire (Oxfordshire Safeguarding Board, 2015). These deeply troubling reports highlighted a long-standing historic criminal activity that had not only profoundly affected many girls (now adult women), but was also an ongoing danger. Critically, the reports highlighted the repeated failures of agencies that should have done more to protect these girls, including police forces and local authorities.

Nearly nine out of 10 children's social care respondents to our survey had observed an increase in referrals where CSE was a concern. Local authorities and LSCBs had responded by strengthening their referral processes and developing a range of materials and training for schools and other agencies to help them to identify and respond appropriately in cases where a young person could be at risk of, or suffering from, CSE. Over four fifths of local authorities had a dedicated CSE team and the majority of these were using a specific CSE risk assessment tool. However, children's social care staff we interviewed acknowledged that this remained a difficult area for schools to deal with, and there were uncertainties about schools' confidence in doing so and the adequacy of support offered to them. The representative of a voluntary sector agency working to support children and families affected by CSE highlighted a case where a teenage girl thought to have been the victim of CSE had been isolated within school to protect her from boys attending the school who were thought to be associates of her abuser. This case had been judged not to meet the threshold for a response from children's social care services.

At the time of our interviews there was a growing awareness of child criminal exploitation (CCE) following widespread media reporting on gang violence and the development of the 'county lines' model of illegal drugs distribution. This model involves organised criminal gangs developing networks connecting urban centres of the drug trade with other regions and towns across the UK. It commonly involves the exploitation of children and young people who are groomed and/or coerced into setting themselves up as drug dealers or suppliers in unfamiliar towns. These gangs invariably target the most vulnerable children and young people, including those living in poverty, suffering from family breakdown, or who are known to children's social care, including young people in care (National Crime Agency (NCA), 2018). Greater awareness of this pattern of criminal activity had opened up a new area of work for local authority safeguarding leads concerned about the potential implications for schools. One education safeguarding adviser commented:

'I am going to have to do a lot of work on that with the schools this year, because I don't think most of my schools have even heard of criminal exploitation. They know they have got pupils who are in hiding or drug carrying or, you know, being mules or whatever. They know that some of their young people go missing and then get picked up by the police. But I don't think there is any understanding that this is organised crime and that it's the same grooming process as sexual exploitation. Even as trainers we were all sitting [in a meeting] going, "bloody hell, we have missed something here".' (Education adviser, metropolitan borough)

Other participants felt that many schools were now both more aware and eager to address this danger to their pupils. However, they also thought that some schools did not want outside agencies coming in and talking about gangs in case they were seen to be encouraging or glamorising them.

Preventing radicalisation

Protecting children and young people from extremist ideologies, radicalisation and being drawn into terrorism has also been added to the list of specific safeguarding concerns schools must now address (DfE, 2021a). Section 26 of the Counter-Terrorism and Security Act 2015 places all staff in schools under a duty to have 'due regard to the need to prevent people from being drawn into terrorism' (the 'Prevent' duty). Under this duty DSLs should consider referring information about individuals they may be concerned about to the Channel programme, which aims to provide 'early stage' support to people who are identified as being vulnerable to being drawn into terrorism.

Through our survey of education safeguarding leads we found that three quarters of authorities employed a dedicated Prevent officer to work with schools. These officers delivered or arranged the Workshop to Raise Awareness of Prevent (WRAP) training. This training was generally attended by DSLs, who were then responsible for ensuring all other staff within their school were appropriately trained. Education leads that we interviewed knew that some schools brought in external trainers to deliver this training to all teachers but thought that it was more common for schools to rely on online training modules. In general, survey respondents from education, children's social care and LSCBs considered schools' knowledge of Prevent to be high and believed that schools were generally satisfied with the way in which their concerns about different forms of radicalisation were handled.

However, this optimism was not reflected in our interviews with specialists working in the area. Two police officers we interviewed were concerned about the implementation of the Prevent duty, which was still relatively new at the time. From their perspective Prevent training had been put in place very quickly and staff in schools had yet to develop sufficient experience in identifying potential radicalisation. An expert on the Prevent programme also commented on how the high profile of radicalisation, combined with a lack of experience and nervousness among school staff, was leading to unwarranted referrals:

> 'So, we have schools (and others) occasionally making a referral about a young person who has converted to a new religion and then becoming more and more devout and they are praying and they are saying provocative things. But actually, it's nothing extremist. There is no hatred and there is no violence and there are no mental health concerns and nothing to suggest they are vulnerable. They are literally a teenager experimenting or finding new things to engage them as lots of young people will do – as with politics or drugs or new relationships or another obsession.' (National Prevent expert)

Furthermore, while media attention at this time focused predominantly on Islamist extremism, experts and local authority staff alike were anxious to make it clear that radicalisation was a much broader problem. In some areas, activities relating to extreme right-wing ideology or animal rights groups were of greater concern. Reflecting these concerns, in December 2019 it was reported that individuals referred to Prevent over far-right extremism had matched those referred for Islamist extremism (Dearden, 2019).

School referrals to children's social care

Under section 47 of the Children Act 1989 children's social care services must initiate a 'child protection' investigation when there are reasonable grounds to suspect that a child or young person is suffering, or is likely to suffer, 'significant harm'. A broader responsibility to promote and safeguard the welfare of children 'in need' is set out under section 17 of the same Act. However, cases referred for consideration will only trigger such interventions if they are deemed by children's social care services to meet the local 'threshold', a decision that referring agencies may not always agree with. Baginsky (2007) found that on many occasions schools were left frustrated when cases they had referred were judged not to meet the threshold for either child protection or child in need, while children's social care staff felt that school staff did not always understand local thresholds and were often making inappropriate referrals. However, in the years since this research was carried out, we have seen the development of both multi-agency safeguarding hubs (MASHs) and policies designed to improve the communication between those with responsibility for protecting and safeguarding children. Furthermore, all local areas are now required to publish their local threshold document (DfE, 2018a). This section considers what our interviews and surveys told us about the impact of these changes from the perspective of local authorities and others in the field before we reflect on the experiences of schools in Chapter 5.

Almost all education safeguarding leads we surveyed confirmed that a MASH now operated in their area. The MASH is a multi-agency team set up to respond to safeguarding inquiries and advise agencies, including schools, about what action needs to be taken in cases where concerns about the safety of a child have been raised. This helps to address the perennial problem of poor information sharing between agencies that has been highlighted in successive Serious Case Reviews, as well as in wider research and policy reviews, stretching back over several decades. The prevalence of these arrangements is in sharp contrast to the earlier study, when the three local authorities involved used call centre staff to handle referrals to children's social care, including one where staff were expected respond to these alongside calls to all other council services (Baginsky, 2007).

Although the precise configuration of each MASH can vary, staff are drawn from a range of agencies, which can include the police, children's social care, probation, housing, youth offending, health and education services. By pooling professional expertise and intelligence, the aim is to generate better risk assessments of cases notified to the MASH at an earlier stage.

This can spur faster responses in cases where children are judged to be at immediate risk of significant harm, but also alleviate pressure on children's social care services by filtering out unnecessary referrals (Crockett et al 2013; Home Office, 2014; Dunne and Finalay, 2016). In nearly three quarters of authorities surveyed education was represented in their MASH and in most cases the education service was funding that position. The benefits for school staff of being able to talk through their concerns with someone with an educational, and preferably school, background emerged in our interviews with local authority staff.

Children's social care managers have also taken other steps to improve their referral systems and to encourage better understandings by schools of what constitutes harm and the threshold at which children's social care would become involved. In many areas this has included the establishment of DSL network meetings to facilitate improved dialogue between schools, children's social care and other safeguarding agencies, although these are not new and were mentioned in the earlier study. In one authority school staff were given the opportunity to spend a morning with children's social care colleagues to observe how they handled referrals and to meet the social workers involved:

'Having been a head in the past and coming from a school background I know I felt that social care colleagues wanted to manage things down, push it back, keep it in your bag – rather than open the door and say this is a problem we all share, and we want the best outcome for children so how do we manage it? We do it by building trust and relationships and by everyone having a good understanding of thresholds.' (Education safeguarding adviser, London Borough)

Among the education safeguarding leads and children's social care managers we surveyed most identified clear thresholds as the most important facilitator of multi-agency working between schools and children's social care services. Amongst the three local agencies we surveyed across England (education, children's social care, LSCBs) almost all confirmed that threshold documents were included in DSL training and the education respondents rated schools' understanding of thresholds as either high or moderate. However, disagreements and misunderstandings between schools and children's social care services in relation to referrals and assessments remained commonplace. Despite their confidence expressed about schools' understanding of thresholds, nearly three quarters of education safeguarding leads identified confusion and/or lack of transparency around the assessment process as a barrier to multi-agency working.

To some extent this was confirmed during interviews with children's social care managers, who thought that the evidence they received from schools was sometimes of such poor quality that it made it difficult for them to make a decision on a case. They also highlighted occasions where they thought that schools had made referrals that were based on low-level concerns simply to 'test the water'. An experienced trainer who had worked with schools across England also questioned schools' understanding of thresholds, contradicting the perceptions collected through the surveys. Despite the reshaping of multi-agency working arrangements already described, we came across only one example of any routine analysis of the number and quality of referrals being made by schools. In this instance, schools were provided with feedback on the quality of referrals and on outcomes in an attempt to improve practice, and it was surprising to us that the approach had not been adopted more widely.

Once again, it is important to reiterate that these changes have been implemented in the context of austerity, which has resulted in more families living in poverty, reduced funding for a wide range of welfare services, and contributed to intense demand pressure on children's social care services. Hood et al (2020) found that some authorities have felt compelled to implement 'demand management' processes to screen out lower-level referrals at a time when social worker vacancies and turnover remain high. This pressure on children's social care was recognised by those we spoke with. However, while 44 per cent of those in LSCBs and education thought thresholds for section 47 referrals (child protection) had risen between 2012 and 2017, only one third of those in children's social care thought this was the case. As far as thresholds for section 17 referrals (child in need) were concerned a similar proportion (44–46 per cent) of respondents in all three agencies thought they were higher. On the other hand, children's social care survey respondents strongly believed that schools were satisfied with the responses they received to both section 47 and section 17 referrals, while education safeguarding and LSCB respondents were far less likely to agree with this. The evidence presented in Chapters 5 and 6 based on our case studies in schools also contradicts this optimistic view and suggests that children's social care staff may have become more accustomed to rising threshold levels, or that they lacked an organisational memory to compare current and past thresholds.

Schools and early help provision

To understand fully how local authorities have responded to financial, workforce and demand pressures, and to begin to form a picture of how this has affected multi-agency working involving schools, it is also necessary to consider the recent evolution of early help provision nationally. On a continuum of support, where tier 1 refers to universal support offered to all children and families, early help is sometimes referred to as 'tier 2' support. The Social Care Institute for Excellence (2012) explains that while 'terminology and boundaries between tiers vary slightly across England, tier 2 services include targeted services for children and families beginning to experience – or at risk of – difficulties, for example school counselling, parenting programmes, support for teenage parents and so on'. Moreover, it is distinguishable from tiers 3 and 4, which refer to more complex interventions, including child in need and child protection interventions. *Working Together* (DfE, 2018a) requires local authorities to publish details of the local early help offer and assessment process as part of the local threshold document. The statutory guidance, *Keeping Children Safe in Education* (DfE, 2021a) requires schools to identify children and families that might benefit from accessing early help provision and liaise with other agencies in carrying out a formal assessment.

The term 'early help' became the preferred term for this level of provision following the Munro Review of child protection (2011) commissioned by the Conservative-led Coalition Government, but its philosophical basis can be traced back to the landmark Seebohm Report (1968), which paved the way for the creation of local authority social services (see Chapter 2). This report envisaged a family-oriented service that would 'reach far beyond the discovery and rescue of social casualties' (Seebohm Report, 1968, para 2). This vision is clearly present in section 17 of the Children Act 1989 (Edwards et al, 2021). However, in the context of significant funding reductions, government policymakers have been reluctant to set out the requirements of early help provision locally in any detail. This reluctance was evident in the government's rejection of Munro's (2011) recommendation that local authorities be placed under a statutory duty to work with partners to ensure sufficient early help provision (Purcell, 2020). Moreover, in the absence of any national data collection requirements, as are in place for tier 3 and 4 provision, it is difficult to form a picture of early help provision nationally. The limited evidence that is available points towards significant variability in the resourcing of early help and an absence of common protocols for assessing and categorising cases (Ofsted 2015b; Lucas and Archard, 2021). This was reflected in responses to our surveys. While many thought that early help provision had increased in their area during the previous five years, just as many thought it had decreased or stayed the same.

But the interviews and comments attached to the surveys contributed to a more nuanced understanding of what was happening with early help in different local areas. To meet financial savings targets and respond to demand pressures, local authorities have worked with partner agencies to redesign services. In some areas it was apparent that the overall early help offer had been reduced. However, other local authorities had prioritised and strengthened the development of their early help offer by encouraging closer working between children's social care and schools and other agencies working beneath the child in need threshold. A key component of this closer working has been the updating of assessment and case management processes at the early help level, replacing or adapting those introduced under the ECM programme, including the Common Assessment Framework (CAF) and the lead professional role (see Chapter 2). Such changes have facilitated a shift towards more targeted early help in some areas. But they have also contributed to the 'demand management' of children's social care services by providing new mechanisms to screen and hold back cases that might otherwise have been referred to children's social care (Baginsky et al, 2019; Hood et al, 2020).

However, unlike at the child protection level, parents cannot be compelled to cooperate at the early help level, which can make it difficult for schools (and other agencies) to secure parental engagement. Moreover, participants acknowledged that the restructuring of early help provision has placed greater responsibilities on schools. At a time when more families were facing financial difficulties, and more children were being affected by parental substance misuse, domestic violence, mental ill-health and other related problems, schools had come under greater pressure to safeguard and protect the well-being of children, especially those serving the poorest communities. Education leads pointed to examples of where schools were increasingly required to deal with complex cases for which they did not feel adequately resourced or qualified, and where they had been required to step into the lead professional role with its responsibility for coordinating multi-agency support for children and families. Reflecting on how schools felt about the new early help arrangements in their area, one respondent to our survey commented:

> 'Many schools contribute significant resources to their families in the form of family support workers, providing food for children, transport when there are difficulties getting to school and becoming involved in extremely complex situations. They are frustrated on occasion when referring to the Targeted Help panel when they believe the family has complex needs that cannot be met by school alone and additional services are not available. It is a challenge for schools with populations of complex need to manage their many lead professional functions in a climate where schools are also required to balance the need to provide representation for statutory functions.' (Education safeguarding lead, unitary authority)

As external services come under pressure there was some discussion in the interviews with sector experts that schools may seek to find their own solutions, which was said to be particularly evident in the number of counsellors that schools were now employing. But there were concerns that without an understanding of the different approaches used by counsellors, schools could occasionally be exposing children to inappropriate interventions:

'I've seen it with an art therapist and I've said to schools, when you're referring children to your school-based art therapist, have you checked out whether art therapy is the right kind of clinical intervention for the kind of problems that the child's displaying? You need to give thought to the evidence base and what works and also that you're not doing something that's more unhelpful than helpful.' (Social care lead for safeguarding, London Borough)

The consequences of not providing support at the right time were described by a youth worker working in a voluntary sector organisation. They highlighted how some schools felt compelled to exclude some pupils because they could not access the support needed to keep them in school:

'I think, by default, our sector is picking up on a huge number of young people with really quite serious mental ill-health, not always very well equipped to deal with it. And what we're having real issues with are when schools are saying this young person is having a psychotic episode, it is not safe for them to be here, it is not safe for other children for them to be here. But when they don't get a response, they are likely to resort to permanent exclusion.' (Youth worker in voluntary organisation)

However, the sustainability of a model of working that requires schools to soak up more pressure was arguably the most fundamental concern raised. As one education manager commented,

'If your budget's reducing and you're losing your pastoral staff and teaching assistants – you're focusing just on teaching, how do you pick up that early support element? But if you don't pick up that early support element, the kids aren't going to be attending school ... you're not going to get your attendance targets, you're not going get your GCSE results and your kids are struggling, and then that just increases your referrals.' (Head of education, metropolitan borough)

Reflections on the multi-agency working revealed in the study

Anne Edwards, Professor Emerita, Department of Education, University of Oxford

This chapter gives rise to both hope and despair. Hope comes from the efforts of highly engaged concerned professionals and their creative responses to challenges detailed in the chapter. Despair is due to the picture of underfunded and overstretched services tackling problems made worse by austerity-driven social policies. Setting the current situation alongside the child-centred ambitions of, for example, ECM initiated in 2003 and the 2011 Munro Review of Child Protection shows so clearly what might have been.

The overwhelming impression from the analysis is the disappearance of the multi-agency working being developed across the England in the first decade of this century. At that point many directors of children's services in England were eroding professional silos to reconfigure children's services for joined-up responses to the complex problems presented at both tiers 2 and 3. Simultaneously, the expertise of practitioners was slowly being enhanced with emphases on working relationally and collaboratively across professional boundaries. These changes needed time to take root and schools were not always keen to join in; Margaret Hodge, then the responsible Minister, observed in 2004 that it would take 10 years. Progress came to a halt in 2010; but we should not forget that progress was possible.

This chapter shows that the meaning of multi-agency working has now changed. When I was researching its emergence in the voluntary sector (Edwards et al, 2006) and across statutory services (Edwards et al, 2009), key ideas were collaboration at a practitioner level and partnership at the local and organisational levels. These words have now disappeared: referral and reporting replace collaboration and the bureaucratic levers of Ofsted and local audits replace partnership.

The findings presented in this chapter have shown that reductions in funding have led to mainly firefighting and dealing with crises in children's social care and the loss of pastoral staff in schools, with schools reporting working beyond their capabilities with tier 2 problems that border on tier 3. It was therefore unsurprising that each sector was concerned about interpretations of the threshold between tiers 2 and 3. These tensions are important warning signals if safeguarding is to be secure.

Training is also a problem. Munro (2011) made much of social work expertise and the importance of professional learning, while we emphasised both for all involved professions (Edwards et al, 2006; 2009). The current reliance on one-off online sessions and cascaded training in schools alongside Ofsted inspections that focus on protocols and paperwork leaves one wondering whether professional expertise is valued and whether skilled responsive and relational inter-professional work with vulnerable children has disappeared.

But there is hope. The energy, care and sense of professional responsibility of the study participants should be celebrated and academisation has not completely broken ties between schools and local services. Last, but not least, the analysis in this chapter exposes a system with so much variation across authorities and these findings raise questions of entitlement and the rights of children to be supported by society. It should be hard to avoid these questions.

PART II

Schools' perspectives

4

How schools are responding to safeguarding and the challenges they face

Introduction

In this chapter, and the two that follow, we consider the developments in multi-agency safeguarding work described in the previous chapter from the perspective of schools, drawing on interviews with over 200 staff in the 58 schools we visited. As explained in Chapter 1 these schools were based in five local authorities across England and in one MAT. The MAT covered several local authorities but was not represented in any of the five study authorities. The five authorities are labelled as Middle County, London Borough, Northern Unitary, Northern City and Rural Unitary and further details about them are in Chapter 1 and Appendix 2. We start by considering what we found out about the DSL role in the schools we visited, including their experiences in the role; the support provided by deputy DSLs and 'safeguarding teams' in the school; the time allocated to the role; and the training and support they had received for their role. In the sections that follow we discuss training provision for all other staff, and the role played by school governors. Finally, we reflect on these schools' overall experiences of multi-agency working. This sets the scene for a detailed exploration in Chapter 5 of their experiences of making referrals to children's social care and in Chapter 6 the roles they were playing in the provision of early help support. In the final section of this chapter we summarise how schools regarded the changing nature of their safeguarding responsibilities and how they were responding.

Designated Safeguarding Leads

All schools must appoint a senior member of staff to the role of DSL to take the lead on safeguarding and child protection, which must be part of that person's job description (DfE, 2021a). During the scoping interviews the local authority education officers had commented on the high turnover of DSLs in their areas and how this impacted on the level of expertise and experience that was available in schools. We were therefore interested in finding out about the experience of the DSLs in our case study schools.

Table 4.1: Number of years' experience of DSLs interviewed

1–3 years	3–5 years	5–7 years	7–10 years	>10 years
19	13	12	8	6

The experience of the DSLs

The length of time the 58 lead DSLs had been in post in these schools is recorded in Table 4.1. While it reflects the reasonably high level of experience across this group it is an understatement as many had been deputy DSLs before assuming their current role and a few had held the role in previous schools. As far as the schools in this study were concerned, the DSLs with the most experience were found in Northern City, with an average of eight years, and those with least experience, with an average of three years, were in the MAT. The MAT figure is not surprising given that several of its schools were new or had recently joined the MAT, a transition that had been accompanied by some staff turnover.

The overwhelming majority of DSLs were senior teachers. Those that were not had progressed to senior management through behaviour and support roles or had been recruited from another sector for their experience as, for example, in the two primary schools where the DSLs had previously been social workers.

Deputy DSLs and safeguarding teams

Although schools must have a DSL, the *Keeping Safe in Education* (DfE, 2021a) guidance leaves it up to schools to choose to have one or more deputy DSLs. Most schools in the study had at least one trained deputy DSL, with all schools in the Northern Unitary and in the MAT having at least one deputy. Where a deputy is appointed, that person must be trained to the same standard as the DSL but, while activities can be delegated to a deputy DSL, ultimate responsibility lies with the lead DSL.

Furthermore, most schools referred to a 'safeguarding team', usually comprising head teachers, DSLs and deputy DSLs. In secondary schools, safeguarding teams usually included heads of year or heads of house. Other staff with pastoral responsibilities such as Special Educational Needs Co-ordinators (SENCos) and welfare workers were also included in these teams. The establishment, or expansion, of safeguarding teams reflects the broader scope of safeguarding work and the additional responsibilities that have been placed on schools over recent years, as described in Chapter 3. In the earlier study (Baginsky, 2007) the head teacher in a primary school was usually the DSL and in secondary schools this role was usually held by one of the deputy head teachers. While this was still the most common arrangement, the prevalence of deputy DSLs and the presence of wider safeguarding teams meant that the intense pressure that could arise did not necessarily have to fall on one member of staff.

Dedicated time for the DSL role

In most schools DSLs were balancing their responsibilities with teaching or a wider welfare remit. In just under a quarter of schools, spread evenly across the case studies, did DSLs have any dedicated time for safeguarding/ child protection. It was estimated that safeguarding/child protection took up 15–100 per cent of their time, although it was also said to vary from day to day and week to week, and to depend on flexibility of, and support from, colleagues. Generally, in those schools dealing with the highest volumes of safeguarding concerns, DSLs were not required to teach or had only very limited teaching responsibilities There were clearly more demands where a higher proportion of the pupil population came from families that were in contact with children's social care and other agencies, but the demands made on DSLs were unpredictable wherever they were based:

'I said to the staff at the meeting on Thursday of last week, this time last year, I had 26 referrals; this time last week, I had 97.' (DSL, primary, maintained, London Borough)

'Some days it can be your whole day, or two or three days as a block, and that literally takes up the whole of your time, and then you might go a few days without [anything].' (DSL, primary, voluntary aided, Northern City)

There could also be implications for other staff, such as where a secondary school head teacher said that:

'Most of the time commitment is located with the DSL but if there is a complex case it takes over and can go from five to 80 per cent ... you can't plan for it, so everything I've planned in terms of my work this week could be thrown tomorrow by a high threshold child protection issue, so I've got to drop everything in order to deal with it.' (Head teacher, secondary, voluntary aided, Rural Unitary)

When asked to reflect on the nature of their role the main message was that however good the training might have been, it was difficult to prepare anyone for the role and that experience was the key factor. One DSL had the opportunity to overlap with her predecessor before assuming full responsibility and valued what she had been able to learn during that period. Others realised that they had gone into the role not knowing what it would entail and, although some had struggled in the early days, they believed that their prior experiences and/or inner strength had enabled them to thrive in the role. However, there were comments that it was not a role for everyone, whatever their seniority, and a few suggested that it would be better suited to someone with a different professional background from a relevant field, such as social work or social care: "You have to have a fundamental understanding of what the education system is, but you don't necessarily need to be a qualified teacher to do that" (DSL, primary, London Borough).

Training and support for DSLs

Keeping Children Safe in Education (DfE, 2021a) specifies that DSLs should undertake training that will give them the knowledge and skills to carry out their role and that this should be updated every two years. Some of those seen during the scoping stage considered it was good practice to evidence such training annually. All the DSLs and deputies we interviewed were at least satisfied with, and often complimentary about, their initial training and about the regular updates and sessions on specific areas such as Prevent and Online Safety.

Four of the five local authorities provided initial DSL training through their LSCBs. The fifth area – the London Borough – signposted new DSLs to private providers and a national charity, but provided specialist training on a range of topics, including updates for DSLs, all of which was well regarded. However, some DSLs would have preferred to have been with other DSLs for their initial training, both for immediate support while they were new in the role and to form a network they could turn to if they needed advice or just a sounding board. All the academies in these five local authorities used the local authority training for DSLs but where they were part of a MAT, they were usually able to access additional or supplementary training. All the schools in the sixth site, the MAT, had all attended training provided by the local authorities where they were based. That MAT also had a safeguarding lead who arranged an annual update event, in addition to ongoing support.

Although participants were generally satisfied with the training offered to them, there were a few suggestions regarding additional areas where they would have welcomed training. These included requests in relation to multi-agency work and, particularly in the initial stages in the role, guidance on attending and contributing to multi-agency meetings. One head teacher of a secondary academy in Middle County suggested that it would be helpful to cluster schools for training and adopt a more tailored approach that took account of schools' populations and their specific challenges. This head teacher had considered using a different provider but worried about both how this would be perceived by the local authority and missing something significant in relation to local practice. Several of those interviewed had been to conferences and sessions run by independent training providers and had found them useful, but they were supplementary to training received from the local authorities where they were based and where local policies and procedures had been covered.

There were comments from a minority of DSLs, as well as other school staff, about the emotional toll of this work. For example, one deputy DSL reflected on the stress under which she and a colleague operated:

'I have taken antidepressants because of the level of anxiety that safeguarding brings in schools ... but I've worked with [name] for six years, it's only in the last 12 months she has mentioned to me that she [has] started having anxiety, she's started second-guessing herself about things. It's that emotional anxiety and that emotional responsibility that has a massive impact on your working week.' (Withheld for reasons of potential identification)

In addition to the more extreme accounts such as this, many DSLs who were interviewed referred to situations where, even after training, they had felt unprepared. These included the shock which they felt when they heard what some children had experienced, their concerns when a referral to children's social care was not accepted, and the learning curve involved in attending and contributing to strategy meetings and child protection conferences.

DSLs themselves were also the point of call for other members of the safeguarding and pastoral teams who sought advice and support. In social work, supervision is seen as part of the duty of care which employers owe to their staff, as well as being an integral part of both continuing professional development (CPD) and performance management. Schools have their own processes for conducting appraisals, but supervision has not been a traditional part of their framework, although it is attracting more attention (Carroll et al, 2020; Stokes et al, 2021). London Borough and Middle County were contemplating providing supervision for DSLs, although neither had decided on an appropriate model, while Northern City already had a peer supervision model in place on which training had been provided. Although it was not evident in all schools in Northern City, there were more references in that authority to a process that was more akin to something that could be described as professional supervision than we encountered elsewhere. It was provided by a clinical psychologist and valued by those who were receiving it, but with the proviso that it was not always possible to prioritise and, as a result, in some schools it was only happening once every half term.

Except for the few DSLs who had a social work background and DSLs in Northern City, most DSLs applied a very broad interpretation of what supervision meant. What was included under the umbrella of 'supervision' ranged through general support conversations with colleagues, regular debriefing sessions with the head teacher or deputy DSL and even the governor responsible for safeguarding, and access to an educational psychologist or other professional in the local authority or in the school, sometimes after a particularly difficult or traumatic case. While they might all be useful, regular supervision sessions would provide a safe space to discuss and reflect on specific cases alongside the opportunity to consider any ethical or professional concerns, as well as the impact of the work on themselves and colleagues.

Other sources of support for DSLs were the safeguarding adviser or equivalent in the local authority as well as network meetings, where DSLs came together at an authority or locality level. There were education safeguarding managers or officers in all five areas and, except for the one in Rural Unitary, there were very frequent references to them as sources of support. Similarly, the schools in the MAT, while appreciating the opportunity to network with other DSLs in the trust, welcomed the opportunity to be in contact with other DSLs in the authorities where they were based who would be working to the same local policies and procedures and whom they could subsequently approach for advice and offer mutual support. At the time of the research DSL meetings were happening in three of the five areas – Rural Unitary, Northern City and Northern Unitary – and were attended by most DSLs who were interviewed, although a small number in Rural Unitary were unaware of their existence. In London Borough some DSLs said they attended a network meeting, while others said either it had been disbanded or they knew nothing about it; and in Middle County, although they had existed, they were reported to have stopped. Sometimes deputy DSLs were aware of these meetings but occasionally there was some confusion between safeguarding fora and other groups, such as the LSCB's frontline practitioner group in Northern City, which attracted a broader group of professionals than DSLs.

Training for all school staff

The *Keeping Safe in Education* guidance (DfE, 2021a) stipulates that all staff working in schools should receive appropriate safeguarding and child protection training as part of their induction, and regular updates at least annually. While there were variations across the five authorities and the MAT, in most schools DSLs provided induction and basic-level training for all the staff in their schools, both teaching and non-teaching, as well as the governor with responsibility for safeguarding. Every few years this might be supplemented by a local authority education safeguarding lead or, in the case of the MAT and other case study schools that were part of a MAT, the safeguarding lead from their trusts. Only a handful of schools said they used an online course for this training but there were also references to quizzes and written briefings to accompany the whole-staff training. Several schools followed up with a quiz after requiring all staff to read the most recent version of *Keeping Children Safe in Education*. In some cases, DSLs and/or head teachers had completed a train-the-trainer course to be able to undertake this work, either because they wanted to avoid the cost of commissioning an external training provider or to make sure that any training reflected the circumstances and personnel of their schools:

> '[Now I have done] the train-the-trainer training, I think I will do volunteers as much as possible in a batch, because when it's been online training, some of them find it horrific. I hadn't appreciated, maybe, that we're slightly desensitised to it … it was just awful for them. I think face-to-face training for volunteers is a definite because they were a bit horrified and shocked [by the online training].' (DSL, primary, maintained, Rural Unitary)

In addition, training on specific topics was available for DSLs from all the LSCBs, including on Prevent and exploitation in its various guises. Some schools chose to commission an expert to deliver face-to-face training on these more specialist areas for all staff, while others provided it themselves, either face to face or by purchasing online training. While schools' preference may have been for face-to-face training for their staff, those that used online training said they were balancing available time and costs to arrive at what seemed to them to be the most efficient form of delivery. There were staff who liked it because of the greater flexibility it offered, and, for some, it fitted with their preferred learning style. However, far more said it was a pragmatic and second-best option. Based on their own experiences, as well as on feedback from their colleagues, DSLs and others explained this in terms of the missed opportunities to discuss and contextualise topics and ask questions, with the suggestion that, as a result, the learning was less likely to be embedded.

A few DSLs referred to 'training overload'. They were conscious that they had to find a balance between providing adequate preparation for all their staff and making some immune to the messages by constant repetition. But many DSLs were keen to stress that training went beyond formal sessions – whatever their format – as safeguarding was central to school practice and would, for example, be discussed in meetings to discuss behaviour and progress, as well as being a standard item for some senior leadership meetings and all staff meetings.

Our analysis of the OSC data we collected from staff (reported in Appendix 4) pointed towards differences in the organisational cultures of primary and secondary schools, which may result in additional challenges for DSLs. Staff in secondary schools were significantly more likely than their counterparts in primary schools to expect organisational resistance to new ideas, less likely to feel they had achieved meaningful results and less likely to feel they were provided with the right tools and support to do their job properly.

Governors

The Education Act 2002 defines the statutory role of governing bodies in relation to safeguarding children and requires them to ensure that schools have suitable child protection policies and procedures in place. This includes procedures for safe recruitment and dealing with allegations of abuse against members of staff and volunteers. Ofsted has made clear that there is no exhaustive list of responsibilities and that in relation to safeguarding and other statutory duties governors perform a strategic and not operational role (Ofsted, 2019). Governors need to know and understand safeguarding requirements and the relevant policies and procedures. They must make sure that certain processes are happening, such as maintaining the central register, but they do not need to do them. There are additional responsibilities in relation to MATs, including the responsibility to ensure that a senior member of the trust is appointed with trust-wide responsibility for safeguarding. It is up to a governing body to decide how they fulfil their strategic and monitoring functions, usually by giving individual governors responsibility for specific areas. All the schools in the study had a governor with responsibility for safeguarding and child protection. Where DSLs provided a view on the designated governor role it was overwhelmingly positive in terms of having someone who could provide objective advice and scrutiny and who was generally regarded as a 'critical friend'. The only exception was in a school where the governor had not attended any meetings and had been removed from the role.

Only 12 designated governors and one chair of governors were interviewed across the 58 schools. No governors were seen in Northern City and no trustees in the MAT schools. One possible reason for the low number was that the visits to the schools were during the day so some governors would have been at work and/or had other commitments and so were unable to attend. The invitations were distributed by the schools so the researchers were not able to encourage attendance. Of this group of 12 governors, five were teachers or head teachers, mainly retired, and one was a social worker. There was also another governor, who was currently teaching in the school, who attended a group interview and so was not seen separately. However, the fact that they held the safeguarding role seemed to be contrary to an ability to be able to monitor what was happening and provide challenge as necessary to their colleagues.

Two of the key elements of safeguarding in schools are the processes around safer recruitment – being clear about the checking and vetting processes around recruiting staff – and managing allegations against staff. All the governors interviewed were clear about these responsibilities and processes, as, incidentally, were school staff. Those who were interviewed also provided interesting reflections on how they assessed their more general contribution. Most stressed the sensitivities and responsibilities that went with the role, but also the support they could provide to head teachers and DSLs. A very experienced retired head teacher said they would advise any head teacher to be cautious about the appointment and to consider the benefits attached to having a designated governor with an appropriate professional background. Given this feedback it was surprising that there was considerable variation across the schools in the expectations of the training designated governors would undertake, ranging from all-staff briefings to three-day DSL training.

Schools' experiences of multi-agency working

Ahead of the more detailed discussions in Chapters 5 and 6 this section examines what school staff told us in general about their experiences of multi-agency working. First, we consider relationships between school staff and social workers and others in children's social care services, which are clearly central to effective child protection and safeguarding. Second, we reflect on schools' awareness of the role played by LSCBs and their views on the transition to new multi-agency safeguarding arrangements. Third, we consider whether a school's status as an academy made any difference or not to their relationships with other agencies.

Social workers and children's social care services

In relation to child protection and safeguarding, social workers and their colleagues in children's social care were the professionals with whom most school interviewees had contact so it is important to contextualise the data that appear in this section. There were many references to times when things had not worked out well in those relationships, particularly around the response to concerns and referrals, timeliness of contacts and sharing of information and these are explored later in this chapter and in Chapter 5. However, it was striking how many very positive remarks were made about children's social care in general and about social workers specifically. Comments such as "generally things work fine, but there was one case ..." and "I've not really had bad experiences working with children's social care, apart from ..." were often made in passing and often when the interviews had concluded.

Whenever opinions are collected it is wise to bear in mind the research conducted by Nass and Yen (2010), who concluded that almost everyone remembers negative experiences more strongly, and in more detail, than positive ones. Even those making a less than positive overall assessment of children's social care, and sometimes of social workers, frequently commented about the excellent social workers with whom they worked. This reflected a widely expressed view that the success of working with other agencies often came down to the qualities displayed by individuals and the chemistry between professionals, as well as clear agreed policies and open communication. Nevertheless, it is important to examine the areas that, as far as schools were concerned, got in the way of a smooth working relationship with children's social care.

Across all the areas there were comments from school staff about the pressures under which social workers operated, arising from the perception that there had been an increase in the demands made on them. These demands were thought to lead to high caseloads and stressful working environments, which led to many leaving the profession, or at least leaving children's services, which, in turn, produced high turnover of social workers. Two frequently referenced consequences were the recruitment of many inexperienced and newly qualified social workers when child protection and safeguarding were regarded as complex practice areas, as well as introducing at best unhelpful, and at worst damaging, inconsistency both for schools but more importantly for families. There were very few criticisms of the way child protection conferences were conducted, the success of which was usually attributed to the expertise of the conference chairs. However, in the experience of some heads and DSLs the intentions of those attending the conference could be thwarted if, subsequently, the plan was not implemented or monitored as intended or a child was removed from a plan too early to free up social workers' time:

> 'The LSCB has agreed [numerous times] there should be clear step-down process. You can't just close a case to child protection because the city needs to have less children on a plan. We should not usurp procedures just because of the pressures that we're all under in our work. And I don't doubt for a second that social workers are far too stretched in this city, with far too many cases to manage, and are probably pressured into having to make quick decisions that could affect the lives of a child and family, but that's a systems problem rather than [justification for] individual cases being closed.' (Head teacher, special secondary, maintained, Northern City)

One of the disadvantages of not having seen other agencies in this project was that we were given examples of when things had not worked well for schools without the opportunity to consider when schools may have been seen to be at fault by other agencies. This may well have been the case as far as communications were concerned. For example, from a school's perspective an agency's omission to communicate with them could lead to an assumption that they were not well integrated into multi-agency structures. This could, for example, have included a failure to alert a school that a child on their roll was in contact with children's social care or to not provide feedback on the progress of a case. It was the type of irritation that could escalate, especially if it were interpreted as undervaluing the contribution and expertise of school staff. There were occasions when schools had felt their contribution and assessments were at best undervalued and at worst disregarded. There were also reports from some DSLs that they had felt on the edge of a professional network when information had been shared between agencies, but education had been excluded.

Another area which DSLs saw as a potential source of friction was the different working practices of schools and children's social care. Although a few said they would consider attending a child protection conference during a school holiday, this did not usually happen and some questioned whether it would be right to do so. However, they also recognised how this could prevent schools from engaging with other agencies for a substantial part of the year. The approach of holidays and weekends also featured as a major trigger for concerns if children became apprehensive about the additional time they would be spending at home, and this could then lead to referrals to children's social care or to the MASH, discussed in Chapter 5. Social workers can be very critical of schools for making 'Friday/holiday' referrals, accusing them of failing to monitor signs and refer earlier (Baginsky, 2007). The accounts from these schools were of situations where they had not been aware of any prior cause for concern, but then they had been left with no alternative but to refer. They were then faced with a dilemma, if a social worker could not arrive before the end of the school day, of whether to keep the child behind, which could bring them into conflict with the parents, or send them home and risk their being in a dangerous environment. It was in situations such as this that understanding on the part of individual social workers was so important as there did not appear to be any guidance on how to deal with different working hours and conditions.

Furthermore, there were several mentions of DSLs and head teachers becoming so frustrated by the response from children's social care, either because of a delay in progressing a case or because of the interactions with a social worker, that they had escalated this to a senior manager in children's social care. In some instances, experienced DSLs or head teachers had taken advantage of their contacts within the local authority to discuss such concerns informally and resolve any problems.

However, in general, there was an absence of such communication channels between schools and senior managers in children's social care through which DSLs and head teachers could raise such concerns. Consequently, DSLs and head teachers were required to follow more formal escalation procedures, which could have a negative impact on working relationships between schools and children's social care staff.

Schools' awareness of Local Safeguarding Children's Boards

Earlier chapters have referenced the abolition of LSCBs following the enactment of the Children and Social Work Act 2017, which introduced substantial amendments to the Children Act 2004 under which they had been established. LSCBs were replaced by three 'local safeguarding partners' – local authorities, police and NHS Clinical Commissioning Groups (CCGs), representing the NHS (CCGs themselves are being reorganised into new Integrated Care Systems at the time of writing – at the start of 2022). *Working Together to Safeguard Children* (DfE, 2018a) made clear that local Safeguarding Partnerships would be expected to name schools, colleges and other educational providers as relevant agencies and 'achieve the active engagement of individual institutions in a meaningful way' (para 26). Local authorities were required to begin their transition from LSCBs to safeguarding partners in June 2018 and complete the implementation by 29 September 2019. Most of our work in schools was conducted during 2018 and early 2019, during the time when preparations were being made and structures were being established in some early adopters.

Schools' awareness of the role of LSCBs varied. LSCBs were generally associated with the training they provided, newsletters produced and, occasionally, for auditing and advice services: "It is the work [LSCBs do] that takes place in the background, in terms of not just the training, but advising schools on staff conduct, advising schools on safeguarding policies" (DSL, secondary, maintained, Middle County).

One of the criticisms of LSCBs in the Wood Review (Wood, 2016) was the difficulty of achieving a fair representation of schools. This was not raised as a problem by those working in the schools in this study. Particularly in Northern City and Northern Unitary there were DSLs who had represented schools and those who were active in various sub-groups, and it was among those DSLs that the most concern was expressed about the new arrangements:

'One of the frustrations that education professionals feel, I think, is that the new system is a triangular system involving social care, police and health. Obviously, education would say it should be a square system involving us as one of the corners as well.' (DSL, secondary, academy, Northern Unitary)

'It was made very clear from the outset that [whatever] the advice that was coming out from the DfE ... the superintendent of [Northern City] Police, argued very strongly that any multi-agency safeguarding arrangements going forward absolutely had to involve schools, and nobody disagreed with him because we've played an influential role in shaping the direction of the LSCB, certainly in the time, I've been on the LSCB. We're able to give a perspective of how it is on the ground ... and that's always been seen as a very, very valuable contribution.' (Head teacher, special school, maintained, Northern City)

Overall awareness of LSCBs within schools was much higher in Middle County, Northern City and Northern Unitary and across the MAT than in London Borough or Rural Unitary. In the case of Rural Unitary, this was consistent with the findings from our analysis of the national surveys, which had shown 'very low congruence' across the views of education safeguarding leads, children's social care and LSCBs. However, in the case of London Borough we had found 'high congruence' across the three agencies (see Appendix 1). On the other hand, findings from our QCA of the schools' interview data pointed towards a strong relationship between the schools' experience of support from the local authority and their interaction with the LSCB (see Figure 4.1 and Appendix 3 for further details).

Figure 4.1: Local authority support by LSCB

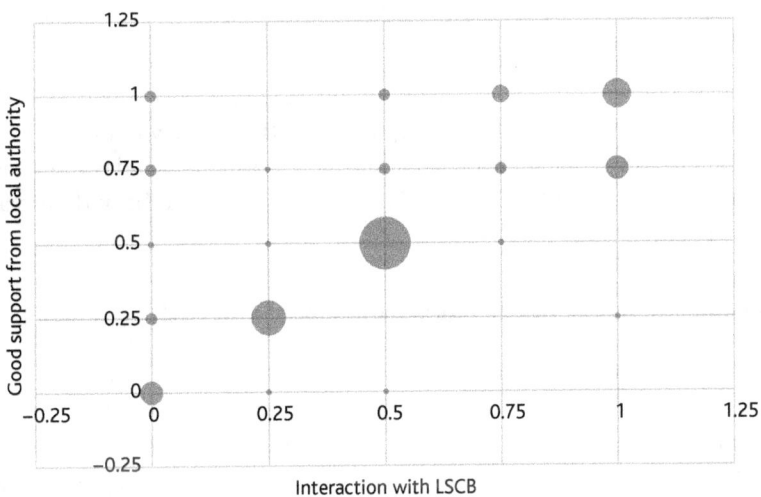

Note: Consistency: 0.88, coverage: 0.74

The impact of academisation

Contrary to what we might have expected when we embarked on this study, it appeared that there were remarkably few differences between the local authority-maintained schools and academies as far as their involvement in and responses to child protection and safeguarding responsibilities were concerned. In most cases the academies in the study viewed the relationship with the local authority very positively and they certainly valued the support, training and advice they were offered. There was just one instance of an academy in Rural Unitary reporting that they had been told they could not have access to particular services because they had not bought into them. This seemed to be a fair response from the local authority, and other academies in the same authority (and in the others) did not report similar problems, probably because they expected to pay for some services, as did many maintained schools. Far more common were responses such as from these two DSLs:

'I've come to work at a free school, but this is much more tied into the local authority than my last school, which was a maintained school.' (Secondary, academy, London Borough)

'So even though we're an academy ... safeguarding still remains with [Northern Unitary], so we would buy into their services, purely because they are the local authority in this area and they still have responsibility ... they are the people that we would liaise with in regard to any child protection ..., so it would make sense to stay with them, rather than to look to any other external providers.' (Primary, academy, Northern Unitary)

The fact that academies and, very often, maintained schools were paying for specific services from the local authority, and could stop this if they decided that they were not meeting their needs or if they could no longer afford them, created a level of uncertainty for local authorities in terms of sustaining services. But, as explored in Chapter 2, this has been their reality for many years.

Schools' views on the changing nature of the task

From the perspective of schools, safeguarding work has expanded in the last decade in different ways, including an increased awareness through tightening of statutory guidance, inspection processes and staff training, all of which have contributed to the rise in identified cases. Many participants reported both increased awareness and confidence among staff as well as a belief that the principle of safeguarding as 'everybody's business' was now well embedded in most schools. The volume of cases in some categories of abuse was perceived to have increased. Across the five areas and the MAT schools staff thought that the overall levels of neglect, domestic violence, and mental health difficulties had escalated. They described how the complex interplay of poverty, homelessness, parental drug and alcohol misuse, child and adult mental health problems, behavioural problems, parenting capacity and skills, and family dysfunction created enormous challenges for management and family support at school level. They linked this with the difficulties they had encountered in reaching the threshold for an intervention by children's social care or to access services from NHS Child and Adolescent Mental Health Services (CAMHS), leaving schools to believe they were expected to shoulder responsibilities beyond their expertise and their resources.

Alongside mental health concerns there were three relatively new areas that were of most concern: radicalisation, CCE and CSE, and online safety, as mentioned in Chapter 3. These are addressed in turn later.

The Prevent duty

Schools varied as to whether they referred concerns they had about cases of possible radicalisation through the MASH or direct to the police. While they were generally positive about the response they received from the former, there were mixed experiences of their interactions with the police. Some reported an overreaction, while others found the response to be sensitive, professional and effective. But there was also concern about the appropriateness of school responsibility for the Prevent strategy, as well as the implications for schools' relationships with families:

'It was a horrible process to go through. We felt as though the family, the parents, turned against us … it was a very delicate situation. … There was always that concern that they were moving schools to get away from us and to get away from being watched. … We felt as though it was a concern that needed to be shared and we were never made to feel that we'd made the wrong decision at all, everyone was really supportive and helped us through it, really.' (DSL, primary, maintained, Rural Unitary)

Child exploitation

When discussing exploitation, participants from schools in London Borough, Rural Unitary and Northern City as well as in the MAT claimed that criminal exploitation related to county lines (NCA, 2018) and/or drug trafficking, and gang activity was now a greater problem than CSE, although they acknowledged the complex interrelationship between the two. Some drew attention to the increased likelihood of CSE in their area being part of wider criminal activities and, while both criminal and sexual exploitation were mainly reported in secondary schools, some primary school participants were proactive in preventative work: "Some of the children have got older siblings who might be involved with gangs, we have to keep an eye on that as well because gangs are romanticised, and [London Borough] has a very high incidence of stabbings and shootings" (SENCo, primary, maintained, London Borough). It was notable, however, that there were few references to sexual abuse, which may suggest that familial sexual abuse is liable to be overlooked in the context of a strategic focus on CSE, a point that has been raised by Ofsted and other inspectorates (Ofsted et al, 2020). Only one participant mentioned the discrepancy between the known statistics and referrals from the school in relation to sexual abuse:

> 'the thing that worries me I think the most is the sexual abuse because I think in all the time I've taught I've had two disclosures ... serious ones ... if you're looking at statistics, it's a lot bigger than that ... people are tending to make allegations years and years later ... what are we missing in primary schools here? What aren't we doing? Is there anything more we can do?' (Deputy DSL, primary, maintained, Northern City)

Online safety

But it was the enormous increase in the volume of safeguarding work arising from the explosion in social media usage in the last decade that was posing the biggest challenge for most schools across the sectors. There was a range of safeguarding concerns associated with social media, from relatively low-level cyberbullying through gaming and sexting to grooming. Their experiences included cases involving extreme violence as well as a range of mental health concerns resulting from inappropriate or harmful online material involving self-harm, suicide and eating disorder sites. Parents – and often staff – could struggle to keep abreast of what was current. Schools had engaged with other agencies and used a range of resources to educate children and parents about the dangers. They had also developed preventative curricula, but the challenge remained overwhelming for many:

> 'We take it very seriously, but ... it's ... trying to knock down a mountain with a little toffee hammer, really.' (DSL, secondary, maintained, Rural Unitary)

> 'There are massive issues with online at the moment, in terms of parents not having a clear understanding of how to keep their children

safe online, and children having more knowledge of technology than parents do.' (Head teacher, secondary, maintained, Northern Unitary)

Many participants drew attention to the fact that very often the harm was incurred out of school hours but was then brought to their attention by students/pupils or parents with the expectation that schools would sort the problem out. Some expressed the view that parents were either naïve or irresponsible in failing to ensure that children's social media activities were adequately supervised or that simple blocks were placed on access to inappropriate sites. It seemed to be increasingly common that parents expected schools to deal with the fallout:

'A dad ... wanted to speak to his child's teacher who is in Year Six, and he said, "I'm very concerned because my child's been looking at online dating websites or sex websites, or looking for information about sex; can you deal with it, please?" Well, yes, of course we will deal with it ... but actually, "what have you done at home that seeks to address it yourself?" And sometimes it very much is about who needs to take responsibility here; is it us? "We will take some part of it, and we will try and support your child with it here, but actually you need to be doing this yourself."' (Head teacher, primary, maintained, Middle County)

However, overall, school staff appeared confident in their practical management of online safety concerns, and more confident than survey respondents had judged them to be.

Mental health

The subject about which school staff appeared least comfortable and equipped to help children related to mental health problems. School staff across the six areas reported increasing levels of mental ill-health among their pupils, ranging from anxiety to self-harm and suicide, which some attributed, at least in part, to the 'exam culture' in schools as well as to societal changes, including access to harmful social media content. Their observations are in line with studies confirming rising rates of mental health diagnoses in children and young people along with increased emotional distress and declining emotional well-being in adolescents, particularly girls (Fink et al, 2015; Lessof et al, 2016; NHS Digital/ONS, 2018; Pitchforth et al, 2019). High thresholds for referrals to CAMHS were reported in all areas alongside long waiting lists. Although some schools were beginning to see slight improvements, participants expressed enormous frustration at the consequences for children's welfare and education and for the impact on schools:

> 'We're seeing more mental health issues than we've ever seen. It's massive, and ... we don't know where to refer students to because there just doesn't seem to be any resources available and ... it just feels that loads of the students are at a real crisis point in their lives and all we can do is fill in a form and record that we've done it.' (SENCo, secondary, maintained, Middle County)

> 'We've got one child ... who has just seen them and has been waiting two years. So, over those two years his behaviour has deteriorated, his progress has gone down. But now that we've managed to access [CAMHS] it's starting to improve ... that's quite frustrating because if you'd listened to us in the first place ... he wouldn't be ... not on track to achieve what he needs at the end of primary.' (Head teacher, primary, maintained, Middle County)

Other frustrations for schools included the fact that missed appointments led to loss of a place on the waiting list, so many schools arranged support to help ensure families attended appointments. In response, schools increasingly resorted to buying in counselling and related services, although some did have access to local initiatives and additional in-school support. As observed in Chapter 6 some schools had addressed these delays by employing more pastoral staff, including social workers or family support workers. While for some schools employing their own specialist support was regarded as a means to avoid the deficiencies of local authority and NHS provision in terms of capacity and consistency of staff, as school budgets came under increasing pressure there was a tendency for support roles to disappear to make sure sufficient teachers were in post. For academy schools, an added challenge was likely to be that if they did not buy in to the local authority's services (such as vulnerable learner services) then a range of potential avenues of support were closed to them.

Schools' response to increased responsibilities

The way in which expectations on schools have shifted in recent years to encompass more early intervention work and greater engagement in more serious cases, as thresholds have risen and the volume and nature of cases expanded, will be explored in more detail in the following chapters. But this shift was viewed by a minority of those interviewed as potentially problematic. There was near universal acceptance that the fact that children spent so much time in schools and that schools know them best meant that schools inevitably play a critical role in safeguarding, and their expanded role in brokering and signposting parents to services was not in the main contentious. Only a minority of school staff regarded this involvement as blurring the line between the role of school staff and what they saw to be the role of social workers; they viewed it as detracting from the core work of schools and considered that it could potentially leave staff feeling ill-prepared to meet expectations. And it was also a minority of senior teaching staff that felt that it was not good use of their qualifications and had found it hard to impress on children's social care that teaching was their core responsibility.

The majority of those seen embraced the challenges they faced and sought to negotiate a role that allowed them to work alongside other agencies, while building supportive relationships with families and the communities they served. Parents, as well as children, were reported to bring a wide range of concerns to school staff, from poverty to domestic violence, gang involvement, sexting and radicalisation. Many of those interviewed believed that building supportive relationships could help arrest difficulties before they became serious and enable school staff to engage effectively with parents should circumstances deteriorate:

'a lot of the strength of the relationships that we have in school prevents things necessarily coming to a child protection or safeguarding concern because parents will engage with you.' (DSL, special, maintained, Northern City)

'Because I've built this relationship up over [time] and things have only just got really bad, it's easy, actually, to have those conversations because she [pupil] trusts me.' (SENCo, secondary, maintained, Rural Unitary)

So, it is perhaps not surprising that some participants were conflicted when they had to raise safeguarding concerns with parents, particularly where it involved a referral to children's social care. For example, where one school became aware that parents were using excessive punishment, the specific circumstances of the case led the DSL and their colleagues to make the decision not to refer to children's social care. That DSL had prior experience of what she considered to be a culturally insensitive and unnecessarily excessive response by children's social care to physical punishment. As a result, the school delayed making a referral in favour of working with parents to change their attitudes and parenting practices. Another DSL was concerned that formal involvement by 'state' agencies not only placed great emotional strain on families, but could also serve to alienate communities that schools had worked hard to engage. Moreover, there was the belief that it was easier for parents to hear difficult news from a familiar and friendly source. If a referral was necessary, most advocated honesty coupled with sensitivity, with one school going so far as to fill the referral form in with parents.

While some parents might acknowledge the necessity of a referral to children's social care it was not always the case. Some schools adopted various strategies to deal with the potential fallout, including ensuring that responsibility for any referral did not lie with the staff member who had most contact with those parents or nominating one member of staff to have 'difficult conversations' with parents so as to try to maintain their relationship with the wider school community. Another concern was the physical and reputational protection of staff, who could find themselves on the receiving end of parental anger, abuse or complaints. Head teachers referred to their responsibility to shield their staff from abuse that may be targeted at them by parents following a referral. As a result, some schools attempted to make sure two members of staff were present if such a situation was likely to occur. There were accounts such as this one describing the level of threat and violence that could be directed towards senior staff:

> 'I don't feel that, really, the pressures upon schools are recognised enough nationally. ... The toll on the school is huge. ... We face those families every single day and we're trying to educate their children, and when the relationships break up because you're having to report things. ... This is quite a violent neighbourhood and we're tackling some of the most violent families, families who are involved in criminal gangs here, so at times ... all of us feel quite threatened.' (Head teacher, primary, maintained, London Borough)

Concluding comments

This chapter demonstrates the extent to which safeguarding is now firmly embedded in the work of schools and is no longer regarded by any but a minority of staff as merely an activity on the periphery of the central business of education. Schools have adapted to that shift and to the volume, urgency and unpredictability of some safeguarding work by introducing a pattern of variously structured safeguarding teams. Chapter 6 describes the expanded early intervention work that schools now undertake and their anxieties around managing cases which do not reach the threshold for children's social care intervention. But the emotional toll on staff and the evidence reported in this and the next two chapters as to the effect of increased pressure on children's social care suggest that serious consideration should be given to the introduction of formal supervision for DSLs in a similar way to that provided to social workers. The What Works Centre for Children's Social Care is currently trialling a model of supervision for DSLs, having run a pilot project in 2020 (Stokes et al, 2021). However, the model used is one developed for social workers[1] and the intention is to reduce the number of referrals made by schools to children's social care. A preferable approach would be to develop a model specifically for DSLs working in schools to provide the support they require rather than adapting a model used with another profession. Support for safeguarding staff to cope with rising mental health concerns among young people is also a priority and will be discussed in the next chapters and in the postscript in relation to the responses to the COVID-19 pandemic.

There are other implications for the status of schools arising from the evidence in this chapter as to the pressures on children's social care and in the context of the financial precipice on which many local authorities now find themselves. First is the question of safeguarding provision during school holidays – a problem hugely exacerbated in 2020–21 as schools closed to most pupils during parts of the pandemic period. Second is the observation that local authorities continue to offer significant support to all schools for safeguarding purposes in line with their statutory duty to safeguard and promote the well-being of all pupils in their local area. The continued relationship between local authorities and academies for this purpose is an important finding of the study, in strengthening a multi-agency approach in an authority. Finally, questions remain as to the status of schools or education providers in the new multi-agency safeguarding arrangements that came into being in 2019 and the extent to which schools feel excluded from or included in local multi-agency discussions.

5

Meeting the threshold: referral to children's social care services

Introduction

As explained in Chapter 3, under section 47 of the Children Act 1989 English local authority children's social care services must initiate an investigation when there are reasonable grounds to suspect that a child or young person is suffering, or is likely to suffer, 'significant harm'. A broader responsibility to promote and safeguard the welfare of children 'in need' is set out under section 17 of the same Act. However, cases referred for consideration will only trigger such interventions if they are deemed by children's social care services to meet the local 'threshold'. Over recent years the establishment of multi-agency fora, policies and practices, both nationally and locally, has aimed to generate shared understandings of different agencies' responsibilities and capacity in relation to child safeguarding. Moreover, all local areas must publish a local threshold document (DfE, 2018a) to make the referral process more transparent and navigable for referring agencies, such as schools and the NHS. But, as the survey results reported in Chapter 3 illustrated, the fact that these documents exist should not lead to the assumption that there is a shared understanding over their contents or interpretation.

This chapter considers the development of multi-agency safeguarding, but within the wider context of rising poverty rates, funding reductions and the demand pressures on children's social care, described in Chapter 1. The first section begins with a discussion of how staff in schools collect and share information about children and families they are concerned about internally and considers the opportunities that existed for school staff to discuss these concerns with children's social care, and other local authority staff before making a formal referral. The second section focuses on schools' experiences of making a referral and the immediate response they received, including their awareness and understanding of threshold documents. In the third section we consider schools' experiences of making a referral to children's social care. The fourth section returns to a discussion of threshold levels for children's social care, building on the discussion in Chapter 3.

Collecting and sharing information within school

Responsibilities placed on schools in relation to safeguarding have grown over recent years as the discussions in Chapters 2 and 3 have demonstrated. In Chapter 4 we showed how the schools that were involved in this research had all allocated resources to meet these responsibilities and it was commonplace to find that DSLs were supported by schools' safeguarding teams, often comprising deputy DSLs who had undertaken full DSL training and who worked alongside other teaching and non-teaching staff with pastoral responsibilities.

Alongside the development of safeguarding teams within schools it was also clear that, for the schools participating in this research, safeguarding was regarded as 'everybody's business'. Participants invariably reported a school ethos under which staff were actively encouraged to report any concern, however minor, to the DSL or the wider safeguarding team. One deputy head teacher commented on the ethos in their school:

'[Staff] are not letting go anything, so although the child says there was a carpet burn and it does probably look like a carpet burn, I'm still going to disclose it, still going to report it. ... So, I think the level of complacency has decreased and people are just on the ball.' (Deputy head teacher/DSL, primary, Rural Unitary)

Some staff interviewed held pastoral responsibilities, for example as SENCos or heads of house in secondary schools, but were not members of the safeguarding team. While they fulfilled their responsibility to report concerns, some found it frustrating that they did not always know how these concerns were being dealt with by the school safeguarding team, nor were they always informed of the outcome. On the other hand, they accepted that sensitive information relating to individual children and families could not always be shared. Moreover, DSLs acknowledged that their colleagues could be left feeling anxious about the safety and well-being of children in their care. The importance of maintaining an 'open door' policy and encouraging staff to talk to them about their concerns was the accepted norm. One assistant head teacher, who was also a deputy DSL, explained:

'Quite often staff members come over next day and say they couldn't sleep, maybe something was disclosed to them, so where it's appropriate, we'll keep them updated on the situation, whether that's somebody else is dealing with the matter or whether it's been resolved. Sometimes if you say it has been resolved they do feel at ease, but we also do offer them a chance to talk to one of the safeguarding leads about what [the safeguarding leads are] going to do, how they're feeling. If we felt that it was a persistent issue for them, then we would refer them to occupational health or if they needed counselling, somebody else to talk to.' (Assistant head teacher/deputy DSL, primary, London Borough)

The implementation of electronic management information systems within schools to record and manage data relating to safeguarding and wider well-being concerns has been an important practice development. Electronic systems were in place in almost half of the schools visited for this research (27 of 58) and were in the process of being set up in a further two. They were more commonly found in secondary schools but were also in place, or about to be implemented, in some primary schools and in one of the special schools we visited. All schools in Northern Unitary used the same system and the local authority had begun feeding information directly into the system, including notifications of domestic violence in any pupil's home. On the other hand, the implementation of electronic recording systems had not been encouraged by the education safeguarding team in Middle County and most schools visited relied exclusively on a paper-based system developed by the local authority. Even so, one school had implemented an electronic recording system and the head teacher at another was considering doing so after talking to colleagues working in another local authority area about the advantages of doing this.

It is the difficulty of managing large amounts of data relating to welfare concerns that has driven the implementation of electronic systems. Given their much higher pupil numbers, this is a particular challenge for secondary schools. However, some primary schools, generally those serving poorer communities, were also managing high volumes of data. One such primary school in Northern City that was planning to implement a new electronic system explained that currently each class had a paper pastoral file where staff were expected to record details such as children not having eaten breakfast or wearing dirty clothes. The value of introducing an electronic system was explained by one SENCo working in another primary school:

'[Before] you just felt like it was lots of bits of paper in a file, whereas with [Online Management System] you've got a really good strong chronology if you want to go back it and look through a child's history. Any actions can be noted, so if you're following things up you can record the action as well, and it's that person, where a piece of paper can get lost or misfiled or anything, but it's definitely a more useful system, useful for passing on information as well to other people.' (SENCo, primary, maintained, Northern Unitary)

This approach helped safeguarding staff trying to assess what they described as the 'whole picture' or to 'complete the jigsaw', in cases where there were multiple incidents and observations, before reaching a decision about making a referral to children's social care.

Support for schools considering making a referral

Baginsky's (2007) earlier research highlighted the value that schools placed on being able to discuss cases with social workers informally before deciding whether to make a referral. In all three authorities in that study some form of call centre had been introduced to handle calls to a whole range of local authority services, including social care. In two authorities this had not prevented schools from seeking advice, however in the other authority the call system operated more formally, and schools reported that it had become more difficult to speak to a social worker directly. Two sources of advice available to schools in our case study areas are discussed in this section: MASHs and local authority education safeguarding teams.

Multi-Agency Safeguarding Hubs

As explained in Chapter 3, the establishment of a MASH in most local authority areas over the past decade has been an important step in attempting to address the perennial problem of poor information sharing between agencies, as highlighted in successive Serious Case Reviews, as well as in wider research and policy reviews, stretching back over several decades. A MASH was in operation in the five local authority case study areas, and in each of the six local authority areas covered by our MAT case study. In general, schools saw the creation of the MASH as a positive development. From their perspective, opening up a dialogue with the MASH, as a single point of contact for multiple agencies, helped staff to reassess their concerns over a pupil in the light of fresh information and provide a sense of whether it was likely these concerns would meet the threshold for a children's social care intervention. One head teacher, who was also a DSL, commented:

'The central point of contact, rather than obviously phoning about five different agencies or having different agencies you have to call – I think that's a real strength of the system … my experience that I've had with the MASH team has been quite positive in terms of how they've reacted to things, the majority of the time … I think it's a good system, I do have confidence in the MASH team.' (Head teacher/DSL, primary, academy, Middle County)

On the other hand, some schools had misgivings about the way in which MASHs operated. One complaint was that the value of phoning it often depended on which member of the MASH answered the call. But a more fundamental concern expressed by some schools was that calling the MASH felt like a formal step because it required detailed information about children and families to be shared and in most cases parents had to be notified about the call. Staff in Rural Unitary, Middle County and Northern Unitary explained that they had previously been able to use the MASH as a more informal sounding board. This head teacher suggested that no longer being able to so could be deterring staff from calling:

> 'When they first introduced it, it was great because you'd ring up for a consultation and that's exactly what it was. ... And my biggest concern around it is ... whereas I might have previously rung for a consultation, there will be times where I won't, because I think actually, if I ring you, I might as well complete a MARF [Multi-Agency Referral] form because I know you're going to ring those parents, and actually I'm ringing for a consultation because I'm not sure whether this is high level enough or not. So do you know what, I'm going to make the decision myself and I'm going to say it isn't.' (Head teacher/DSL, primary, Middle County)

The same head teacher also admitted that on some occasions she would call other head teachers for advice rather than the MASH. Two other experienced DSLs reported sometimes relying on their personal contacts in children's social care to seek advice, even though they were expected to call the MASH initially.

The situation in Northern City was somewhat different, with a new system having been introduced that allowed schools to seek advice from one of three early help hubs where they could speak with a consultant social worker. Previously, schools had been able to call the MASH for advice, but some schools told us that this arrangement had not worked well from their perspective and that regardless of what information was shared they would usually be advised to submit a referral. However, school staff expressed mixed views on the early implementation of the new approach. One primary school DSL felt that this new arrangement was 'much better' because it provided direct access to a social worker, while in another primary school the DSL highlighted what was a perenial complaint across schools wherever they were and that was difficulty of getting hold of social workers, even these consultants in the hub. In the earlier study in 2007 one point of contention between teachers and social workers was the 'Friday afternoon' referral. Teachers said they often became specifically aware of children's fears as a weekend approached even if earlier indications had been present. Social workers had accused teachers of waiting too long and expecting a response at short notice. One DSL in a secondary academy believed that, unless the change was properly resourced, the new arrangements could lead to an increase in the number of referrals, including those on a Friday afternoon, if schools could not reach a social worker for advice on the appropriateness of a referral.

Education safeguarding teams

Most of the local authorities that completed our national survey confirmed that they employed at least one person, and frequently more than this, to provide strategic support to help schools meet their safeguarding responsibilities (see Chapter 3). This generally involved advice in relation to school policies and procedures, and sometimes support with inspection preparation. Many education safeguarding leads also took responsibility for the delivery and/or commissioning of training for school safeguarding teams.

In each of the case study areas schools spoke positively about support provided by education safeguarding teams. Many felt able to turn to their education safeguarding teams for advice regarding child protection and safeguarding concerns in addition to, or as an alternative to, contacting the MASH. As far as schools were concerned the advantage of this was that the advice was offered more informally and, if no further action was needed, then it avoided the need to complete forms and notify parents. Furthermore, in none of the case study areas did we find evidence of separate arrangements for maintained schools and academies. Schools in the MAT case study had the additional advantage of also being able to call the MAT's own safeguarding lead for advice and support, with one secondary DSL commenting that they felt able to contact her day or night, although they probably meant 'evening'. The positive comments made by schools in Middle County and Northern City were also striking, as the following quotes illustrate:

'I think the lead for Middle County in terms of safeguarding, is very, very strong ... lives and breathes safeguarding. We actually have a direct line to him if we have concerns, he will pick up his phone.' (Assistant head teacher/DSL, primary, academy, Middle County)

'We have an absolutely great safeguarding person within the local authority. ... I have spoken to him in the evenings if I've been worried about a case, [and] at the weekends. ... I actually phoned on Friday to just ask for advice, so you never feel on your own; the advice is always there.' (Head teacher/DSL, primary, Northern City)

The referral process

If a case was judged likely to meet the threshold, schools in four of the five case study areas[1] were required to complete an online Multi-Agency Referral Form (MARF) before a final decision was made. The exceptions were those in Rural Unitary, where the MASH operator made notes of the telephone conversation which were passed to children's social care colleagues, which meant schools there were not always required to complete a MARF for a case to progress. However, if a child was judged to be at immediate risk of significant harm, action would be initiated immediately in all case study sites, with the MARF being submitted later if required. This section considers schools' experiences of completing a referral, the role of threshold documents and immediate responses to referrals from the MASH.

Submitting a referral

Schools in London Borough did not see completing a MARF as difficult. One assistant head teacher/DSL in a primary school explained that after the form had been reviewed by the local authority the revised version now took approximately 20 minutes to complete compared with the couple of hours previously needed. However, that authority was the exception and the length of time taken to complete a MARF was raised as a problem by schools in all the other three case study sites where this was required.

Some staff, including this DSL, considered the requirement to complete a time-consuming MARF after a long conversation with the MASH to be unnecessary:

'I feel like sometimes someone on the phone could be filling all of that in, to say, right, okay, you've just telephoned in a referral, we've got all the information we need, off we go. Because sometimes that can add like an hour. By the time I've got off the phone, filled the form in with as much detail as possible, I've sent it to MASH, MASH have then allocated it to children's services and then children's services have picked it up and allocated it to the team. That's quite a long process, whereas actually, they had all of that information from my phone call and that could have just gone through.' (Assistant head teacher/DSL, secondary, academy, MAT)

However, even though the time taken to complete a MARF was frustrating, most staff did not question why they needed to complete it rather than the MASH doing so. One head of year commented:

'Although I don't like doing the MARF forms, they are quite lengthy, I think it's useful to have it written down, because if you just do it over the phone, you don't know how much of what you're saying is being written or typed up, or whatever, how much of that information is getting back to the social worker or to the person who needs that information.' (Head of year 9/deputy DSL, secondary, academy, Northern City)

In Rural Unitary, where schools were not required to complete the MARF, one deputy DSL commented that they would prefer it if the school completed the form:

'because on a phone conversation, you've got someone on the phone, how do you know that they're writing down exactly what you're saying? And I ... personally ... I do like that form, and I know it's time consuming but at least it's your information and if anything was wrong on it, it's you, you did that, but you don't know ... so I do miss that, I do wish they'd bring back that form.' (Family support worker/ deputy DSL, secondary, academy, Rural Unitary)

A deputy head teacher in another secondary academy in Northern Unitary conceded that the way in which the MARF was completed, and the decision to submit the MARF itself, could be spurred by not wanting to "drop the ball" and by "an element of ... arse covering that goes on with safeguarding".

Threshold documents

Baginsky (2007) found limited evidence of shared understanding of thresholds across what were then social services and the schools she visited. Social workers believed that schools were referring too many cases that were below the threshold, while school staff felt frustrated by what they perceived as the high thresholds they faced in getting any response. We were interested to find out if the publication of threshold documents in recent years had helped schools to arrive at a better understanding of local thresholds. *Working Together* (DfE, 2018a), the statutory guidance for professionals across all agencies, states:

The safeguarding partners should publish a threshold document, which sets out the local criteria for action in a way that is transparent, accessible and easily understood. This should include:

- the process for the early help assessment and the type and level of early help services to be provided

- the criteria, including the level of need, for when a case should be referred to local authority children's social care for assessment and for statutory services under:
  - section 17 of the Children Act 1989 (children in need)
  - section 47 of the Children Act 1989 (reasonable cause to suspect a child is suffering or likely to suffer significant harm)
  - section 31 of the Children Act 1989 (care and supervision orders)
  - section 20 of the Children Act 1989 (duty to accommodate a child)
- clear procedures and processes for cases relating to:
  - the abuse, neglect and exploitation of children
  - children managed within the youth secure estate
  - disabled children

We found that approximately three quarters of staff in schools were aware of the existence of a local threshold document. However, this included two DSLs (one in London Borough and one in Middle County) who were aware that it existed but had never seen it. All DSLs in secondary schools were aware of them in the six sites, but only in Northern City and Northern Unitary were all DSLs aware (Table 5.1). However, as we found out, awareness did not necessarily equate with familiarity with its contents or a positive assessment of its usefulness or relevance.

In most of the authorities, it is probably true to say that schools were at best sceptical and at worst dismissive of its relevance, commenting that in practice thresholds were open to interpretation. In Northern Unitary the MASH team had attended the local DSL network meetings to discuss ongoing concerns regarding referrals made by schools despite widespread knowledge of the threshold document. One DSL in Northern Unitary had previously been a child protection social worker and regularly attended these meetings. Based on the discussion with the MASH representatives, she agreed that some schools still did not understand the local threshold and so continued to make inappropriate referrals. Interestingly, schools in Northern City, the other area with the highest awareness of the document, spoke about using it to frame their referrals to maximise their chances of meeting a threshold. Asked about their awareness of the document, one DSL explained:

'Yes, I am very aware of it. It is always discussed in the safeguarding training for Designated Safeguarding Leads. We have the window screen wiper model [sic "windscreen" model]. ... When you complete the [Northern City] MARF online, it asks you whether you're submitting it as child in need or child protection, and it asks you to acknowledge

Table 5.1: School DSLs stating that they were aware of the local threshold document

Case study	Number of schools	DSLs aware of threshold document
London Borough	10	7
Rural Unitary	10	5
Middle County	10	6
Northern City	10	10
Northern Unitary	10	10
Multi-Academy Trust	8	6
Total	**58**	**44**

that you're familiar with that document. And quite often what we will do when we're completing the MARF is evidence our decision about whether it's child in need or child protection by referring specifically to the various indicators under the various levels.' (DSL, secondary special school, maintained, Northern City)

Another experienced DSL in the city, who was also a head teacher, commented that multi-agency training around thresholds and how to complete the MARF meant that her referrals were now usually accepted. However, this comment was an exception, with staff at other schools in Northern City more often complaining about referrals being declined.

Getting a response

As noted earlier, on balance, schools were positive about the contribution of the MASH in their local area. Having a single point of contact to discuss concerns with and exchange information was welcomed. Several schools, across different case study sites, also commented that they were satisfied with how the most serious cases were dealt with, describing how a call to the MASH would spur relevant safeguarding agencies into action, usually within 24 hours: "When there is a concern and it meets their threshold, they can act pretty quickly" (SENCo, primary, Middle County); "Generally, at tier three and four,[2] it's great, it's spot-on" (DSL, secondary, academy, MAT).

On the other hand, some schools, including several in London Borough, highlighted delays in the decision-making process after contacting their MASH. The type of 'Friday afternoon' referrals described earlier were said to be a particular pinch point when many schools made calls to discuss concerns before the weekend or a school holiday. One deputy head teacher commented:

'Friday is always a busy day if you phone MASH on a Friday, because at five o'clock, they go. You could be pulling your hair out and you've got a situation to deal with. I think sometimes it depends who you get on the other end of the phone, and it depends on the manager who's on duty. Some managers will say, "oh, that's got to go straight to child in need", another person say "we'll get back to you" and you don't hear anything, so that's the frustrating element of it really.' (Deputy head teacher/deputy DSL, primary, maintained, London Borough)

Furthermore, many schools across all case study areas found that the response to referrals judged to be less urgent could be slow. Often schools would be left to chase up the outcome of a MARF or to find out about progress after an assessment by children's social care had been initiated. Schools in London Borough also spoke about their negative experiences of attending inter-agency meetings on specific cases, including poor communication by social workers regarding dates and venues, technical difficulties in phone conferences, and not always feeling listened to. On the other hand, schools elsewhere acknowledged that improvements to training and the establishment of multi-agency safeguarding fora had enabled schools to express concerns and that changes had been made. One DSL explained:

'I think the communication with [MASH] is very good. [MASH] have come to our cluster meetings and they've ... schools have been able to say what they were frustrated with and [MASH] have said, this is what ... how we could do things quicker or more effectively, what do you need ... so I think there is a two-way process.' (DSL, primary, maintained, Northern Unitary)

Referrals were one of the areas where QCA (see Appendix 3) was helpful in allowing us to interrogate the data more closely. We found a strong relationship between schools' positive experiences of referrals – where the DSL was positive about referrals in terms of responsiveness/timeliness, communication, actions and feeling engaged/involved in the process – and where they assessed multi-agency working positively – where the DSL mentioned engaging in multi-agency work with several different agencies and reported overall positive experiences. Figure 5.1 illustrates that a DSL reporting a positive experience of multi-agency working is sufficient to assume that the DSL will also have a more positive experience of referrals.[3]

Figure 5.1: Referrals by inter-agency working

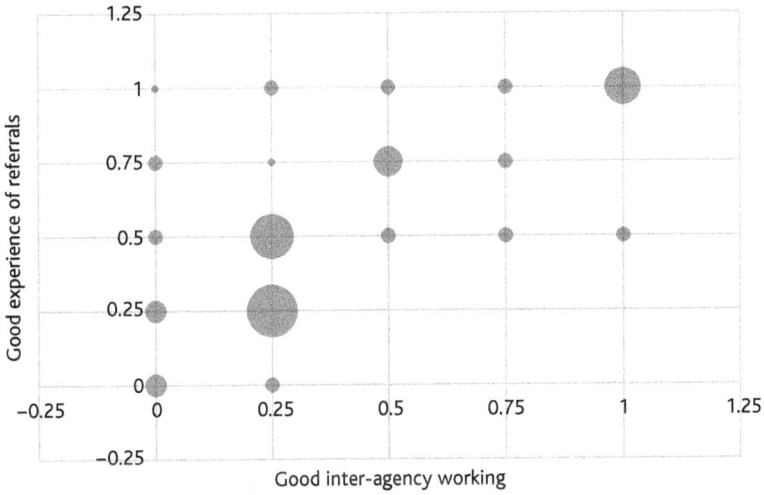

Note: Consistency: 0.9, coverage: 0.64

Of all the combinations of conditions we examined, the most effective in determining whether a DSL would have a positive experience of referrals was that they also had a good experience of inter-agency working more generally.

Rising thresholds

This section considers what schools told us about their perception of threshold levels in their local area and demand pressure on children's social care. It also discusses what happens if a referral is not taken on and what is then expected of schools.

Threshold levels

In the earlier study (Baginsky, 2007) many schools expressed concern regarding the way in which their referrals were dealt with, often feeling that the local threshold was too high. Similarly, in this study staff in schools said they knew that only the most serious cases would receive a response, as these teachers explained:

'It's almost as if you've got to wait for something to go wrong before something happens.' (DSL, secondary, academy, Northern Unitary)

'I think it worries me that so many of our children have gone from nothing to care. That's not right. It's not right. And you know two of those children that have gone out of this city now, I reckon I've probably put in four MARFs that didn't meet the threshold. What does meet the threshold then?' (DSL, secondary, academy, Northern City)

As discussed earlier, schools appeared to be collecting and recording substantial amounts of information about the welfare of children and there was also a greater awareness of the range of safeguarding risks to which children and young people were potentially exposed to which schools had to be alert. However, they still reported that they found it difficult to provide sufficient evidence to meet the children's social care's thresholds, particularly in cases of suspected neglect where evidence had been built up over time, but no single incident had set alarm bells ringing. While neglect is the most common form of maltreatment registered in England (DfE, 2021b), professionals have a problem identifying and acting on indicators of neglect (Laming 2003; Gilbert et al, 2009), a point acknowledged by this head teacher: "I think it's very difficult to prove neglect, and although they're probably the families that we know of the most, nothing is ever quite significant enough for anybody to make a decision and go, yes, actually that meets threshold" (Head teacher, primary, Middle County). This was particularly frustrating for primary school staff who worked with the same children every day and felt well placed to notice changes in the well-being or demeanour of the children in their class. This DSL felt that the closeness of such relationships was not always appreciated:

'I feel that the local authority doesn't place enough trust in the school's judgement … as staff in this school, we see that child every day and we can see that this is an unhappy child. I can't relay that to you on a piece of paper in a child protection referral, but if on that referral I state that having seen and met the child I consider that child is in need of some kind of support. They have to trust my judgement on that as a professional and not go by a tick-box …' (DSL, primary, maintained, London Borough)

Some case study schools, usually in the secondary sector, had pupils who travelled in from two or more different local authority areas. This created additional challenges because children had to be referred to the local authority where they lived, not where the school was located. The frustration faced by those working with different local authorities that seemingly applied differing thresholds is captured in this quote from a head teacher in Rural Unitary:

'I think there needs to be some greater moderation across borders to make sure that kids one side of the street are getting the same deal as the kids the other side. I don't think that's always the case. There's always a frustration over, well why doesn't this meet threshold, and a school view and a social services' view not matching. ... So the biggest problem I think with social care over the last five, six, seven years is, certainly in the two authorities that I'm dealing with, would be a lack of consistency in applying the thresholds.' (Head teacher, secondary, maintained, Rural Unitary)

Demand pressure

The increasing demands made on children's social care were highlighted in Chapter 1 and in the introduction to this chapter. In the context of rising levels of poverty and public sector austerity, the provision of children's social care in some areas may be driven by the pressure to manage scarce resources more than responding to levels of need (Bywaters et al, 2016; Hood et al, 2020). The findings from this research provide some evidence to support that conclusion.

The national surveys we conducted, reported in Chapter 3, showed that safeguarding leads, as well as representatives of children's social care and LSCBs, agreed that local thresholds for section 17 and section 47 referrals were higher, or much higher, than five years previously. When we asked staff in the 58 schools we visited whether there had been changes to thresholds over the past 5–10 years, just under half were able to provide a judgement. In 28 schools, staff in 23 thought thresholds had risen, while the remaining five thought they had stayed the same. A higher proportion of staff in schools in London Borough and Northern City thought that this was the case, which may relate to the fact that they were the two local authorities with the highest levels of poverty.

Although schools were clearly frustrated trying to negotiate children's social care thresholds and failing to do so, it was striking how many of them in London Borough and Northern City, but also in Northern Unitary, acknowledged the demands made of children's social care and the impact this had on its capacity to respond. Several schools in London Borough specifically highlighted the heavy workload of social workers and how difficult it was for the local authority to recruit and retain them. These pressures, combined with those created by diminishing resources, which were most acutely felt in areas with the highest levels of deprivation (Bywaters et al, 2018), reflect the reality that thresholds are shaped by local and national conditions with the attendant consequences for the agencies left to manage them and the children and families that are at their mercy:

'Sometimes it feels like it's very much reactionary [*sic*], or we have to wait until something happens ... to get it through the threshold, through social care, through a MARF, is very, very difficult. So, things that would have been taken up or assessments that would have been completed a few years ago are not happening now, and it's being referred back to school.' (DSL, secondary, academy, Northern City)

'It is very difficult to meet the threshold in [London Borough], that is one of the big problems that we face ... because there are so many cases of neglect in the borough, it kind of almost feels like it's normalised. So, I've always said that, just because a child lives in [London Borough] and they're suffering neglect, doesn't mean that they shouldn't be given the same support as a child that perhaps lives in a different area that's much more affluent, where they would get maybe more support because there's less [*sic*] cases of neglect.' (DSL, primary, maintained, London Borough)

What happens next?

The decision to make and process a referral is not taken lightly by school staff, so if they are told that it has not met the threshold, they may find it frustrating or sometimes alarming. Ofsted's guidance for its inspectors (Ofsted, 2017) at the time of the research advised them to request at the start of the inspection 'a list of referrals made to the designated person for safeguarding in the school and those that were subsequently referred to the local authority, along with brief details of the resolution' (p 28). Inspectors may also check how the referral was made and the thoroughness of the follow-up. Although not mentioned elsewhere, a small number of schools in Rural Unitary and Northern Unitary informed us that they had successfully challenged the outcome of a referral using the local authority escalation procedure or by raising a case with children's social care senior managers. Escalating a concern is a big step for schools, so it is perhaps not surprising that these instances were exceptional. Schools more commonly pursued a strategy of continuing to collect and record information on children and families they had concerns about to inform any subsequent re-referral.

If children's social care did not accept a referral as a child protection or child in need case this did not mean further action was not taken. At that point schools were invariably advised to consider what early help support could be put in place. For most schools this would usually involve completing another assessment to be submitted to a separate team within the local authority. In Northern Unitary the process was different and a single assessment was used for referrals to children's social care and early help, meaning that cases not accepted would generally be passed on to the local authority's early help panel for consideration. Irrespective of any reports or policies that stressed the importance of early help or intervention, many schools felt that it was now harder to trigger a children's social care intervention. Echoing the views of many of those interviewed during the scoping stage, this DSL explained:

'We'd have a lot of different children that would be on child in need plans instead of early help plans, three, four years ago, so actually it's almost like a lot sometimes are dropped into different bands and obviously there's no compulsory family involvement at child in need or below, which can raise its own challenges, and the child in need threshold is continually moving.' (Assistant head teacher/DSL, primary, academy, Middle County)

In the context of cuts to early help, discussed in more detail in the next chapter, schools invariably felt that a recommendation of early help meant that cases were simply being handed back for them to deal with, as the following comment illustrates:

'I get really frustrated and angry sometimes that, when we put referrals in they pass it back to us and we have to deal with it. Even if they've [parent] hit the kid and then they do an assessment and say, it was a one-off, this, that and the other, pass it back to you, you do some work with them, and we just don't have the resources. Whereas before, they used to take them on and do really good work with them, lots of intervention, a variety of different third-party agencies working with them, now it's just ... there's nothing there, and it's the school that's responsible for a lot of things.' (Deputy head teacher, secondary, maintained, Northern Unitary)

In Northern City, one head teacher felt that the pressure on children's social care was also leading to cases being closed too quickly, with social worker support being withdrawn and schools left to deal with cases at early help level:

'It can be frustrating ... because you spend your time following the process to escalate something and it works well and whilst that support is in place ... the family are responding and working and it's the minute it starts working well for them, support starts to go and that's when it's needed the most, to embed that, that learning with the family, really. And we can say, look, we've seen this pattern before; if you pull out now, this will all fall apart and then we'll be escalating again and the whole process starts again from the beginning, instead of sticking with it for a longer period.' (Head teacher/DSL, primary, maintained, Northern City)

Concluding comments

Our research found that schools were very clear about their responsibilities to report concerns about children, as well as evidence of positive developments in safeguarding practice both within schools and at the multi-agency level. As schools' responsibilities in this area have expanded, more resources have been allocated to safeguarding work and most school staff now have a better understanding of the contribution they need to make than was evident when the earlier study (Baginsky, 2007) was conducted. Although not without difficulties, the schools we visited spoke positively about the contribution of the local MASH and/or local authority education safeguarding teams. We also found evidence, through analysis of the interview data, that in areas where DSLs felt that schools were treated as equal partners, were able to access 'most' agencies and regarded communication between agencies as working well, they had better experiences of the referral process. On the other hand, negative experiences of referring to, and working with, children's social care remained commonplace, which sadly echoed the findings of the earlier research conducted around 15 years earlier.

Moreover, reviews of the international literature on the detection and reporting of child abuse (Gilbert et al, 2009; Bunting et al, 2010; Bell and Singh, 2017; McTavish et al, 2017) have also found that it is common for schools to report mostly negative experiences of working with child protection agencies. Is the problem down to one factor? Social workers interviewed by Baginsky (2007) in the earlier study thought that schools did not understand their thresholds and made too many inappropriate referrals. Similar views have also been expressed by staff working in child protection agencies in New Zealand (Beddoe and de Haan, 2018) and Canada (Gallagher-Mackay, 2014). However, nearly all (97 per cent) those in children's social care responding to our survey thought that schools did have at least a moderate understanding of thresholds and over a third (39 per cent) thought it was high.

Our study points towards a deeper problem around thresholds from schools' perspective. First, we found that although threshold documents are widely used, particularly in secondary settings, they are open to interpretation and do not provide schools with a fixed view of where local thresholds lie – although it is unlikely that they ever could do that. Second, the impact of increased pressures on children's social care and the extent to which services had been reduced and rationed were having an impact on schools, which were also facing their own budgetary challenges. It is not surprising that they sometimes felt that they were being used to compensate for these shortfalls and were concerned that cases were increasingly being pushed back to them to devise a solution. These and other findings are considered in the next chapter, alongside evidence of what now seems to be expected of schools.

6

Beneath the threshold: 'early help' and schools' support for children and families

Introduction

Historically schools have played a vital role in promoting the welfare of children alongside fulfilling their educational responsibilities, as discussed in Chapter 2. Although Labour governments between 1997 and 2010 stuck to their pledge to make education their number one priority (Labour Party, 1997), New Labour's policies for children and families were part of the focus on the development of social capital, which was integral to the 'modernization project' or the 'third way' between Conservatism and Socialism (Giddens, 1998; Gamarnikow and Green, 1999). Under the government's ECM reform programme efforts were made to ensure that all schools contributed to multi-agency working in their local areas (HM Government, 2004). With the election of the Conservative-Liberal Democrat Coalition Government in 2010 the key policy commitment, set out in the Foreword to the coalition agreement, was that its budgetary deficit reduction programme would take 'precedence over any of the other measures' (HM Government, 2010). While education policies continued to place a stronger emphasis on pupil attainment and the autonomy of schools vis-à-vis local authorities (DfE, 2010), the broader child welfare agenda was not in evidence. The significant cuts in funding contributed to severe reductions in early intervention services at a time when there was an increased demand for children's social care services. The National Audit Office (NAO) found that by 2014 there had been a 14 per cent increase in the number of children looked after by local authorities (NAO, 2014b). This was the result of several factors but it placed additional financial and workforce pressures on local authorities' children's social care services. Local authorities and partner agencies in the voluntary sector were forced to close and/or restructure local services, reducing the overall offer (Purcell, 2020). However, notwithstanding these shifts in policy and reductions in funding, local authorities are nonetheless required to publish details of the local 'early help' assessment process and the level of services to be provided (DfE, 2018a). The process is intended to address children's needs which require a multi-agency response at an early stage. This chapter discusses how the schools we visited sought to assist children and families under local early help arrangements or by drawing on their own resources.

One of the biggest challenges which schools said they faced, and which was mentioned by most schools in the study, was cases which they often classed as neglect, but which failed to meet the threshold for an intervention from children's social care. These cases were generally viewed as complex and multifaceted, involving the interplay of poverty, domestic violence, substance misuse and parental mental ill-health. As reported in the previous chapter, when a referral failed to lead to an intervention by children's social care, schools were often advised to consider applying to early help services for support.

The first section of this chapter discusses the early help arrangements in place in each of the case study areas and schools' experiences of trying to access these services. The second section considers the views of school staff on taking up the lead professional role, involving responsibility for the coordination of multi-agency early help packages of support for children and families. The third section highlights examples of welfare support provided by or through schools themselves, working outside of local early help arrangements. In the final section Alun Rees reflects on Chapter 4–6 which have focussed on the experiences of the schools we visited.

Early help arrangements

The introduction of the Common Assessment Framework, the Team Around the Child, and the lead professional role under Labour's ECM programme, referred to in Chapter 2, was designed to promote more integrated multi-agency working and a shift towards 'early intervention' to prevent the escalation of problems into children's social care, with the risk that this would be followed by more legalistic interventions, especially child protection procedures. However, as funding for early intervention was cut, central government guidance and oversight were withdrawn or relaxed, leaving it largely up to local authorities to determine how local services are reconfigured to meet savings targets (Purcell, 2020).

In this context, it was clear that schools in all our case study areas were finding it more difficult to access external support following public sector funding reductions. This was reflected in the reported slower turnaround of applications for support and much longer waiting lists for interventions. Some local authorities and voluntary services had also introduced charges for their services to make up for reduced income. Thus, at a time when many schools were finding it harder to meet the threshold for children's social care support and were being told to consider early help, many were finding it harder to access this support. The following quote reflected the experience of many schools:

'There used to be loads of people. We had a list … we had that many, we wrote them all down and put them round the staff room, and the staff room's quite large, and we got round the circumference of the staff room with all these on A4 pieces of paper saying what the service was and what was involved … then all the cuts started and then there's nothing.' (Deputy head teacher, secondary, maintained, Northern Unitary)

The loss of family support workers as these posts were cut was highlighted by schools across the case studies areas, including the following two:

'We've lost that sort of middle tier of the family support workers, the people who would go in and do some work in the home, a short, sharp intervention of, say, six weeks to help with behaviour; "let's pull it down, let's get these consistent patterns happening, let's get the routines", all of those … that isn't as easily accessible anymore.' (Head teacher/DSL, primary, Rural Unitary)

'Trying to get a family support worker is like banging your head against a brick wall, it really is.' (DSL, primary, maintained, London Borough)

Local early help arrangements in London Borough and Rural Unitary required schools to complete a CAF assessment to access support from other agencies, while the other local authorities had introduced a new simplified form of Early Help Assessment (EHA). In Northern Unitary this had been merged with the MARF, designed for referrals to children's social care, to create a single assessment form. Completed assessments in each area were considered by a central early help team or a multi-agency panel that would determine which services, if any, families could be offered or for which they would be put on the waiting list. The replacement of the CAF, reported elsewhere to be a time-consuming and bureaucratic process (Brandon et al 2006; Norgate et al 2009), was broadly welcomed where this had happened. However, as the primary driver for schools to undertake a CAF or an EHA was the likelihood of it resulting in access to services, the more limited the availability of early help services the greater was the reluctance to complete them. As this school SENCo explained, "I do think very carefully about whether I'm going to lead on a CAF, because I'm not going to do one for the sake of doing one. It's only if I think I can get something out of it for the family, I'll do it" (SENCo, primary, maintained, London Borough).

Schools thought that the multi-agency panels in their local area had become less effective in linking schools with agencies best placed to provide early help for children and families. Fewer agencies were participating in the panels as capacity had become more stretched:

'It was always a big CAF network meeting and then we'd take a case there ... but then there were more outside agencies then, so you could easily sit in there and say, "oh, let's get that service to come out, let's get that service to come out", whereas now there's nothing. So [a] CAF wouldn't be any use now ...' (Family support worker, secondary, academy, Rural Unitary)

Multi-agency panels also relied upon local authority employed staff to ensure that they operated effectively. This DSL explained the negative impact of cuts here:

'We have a thing called early intervention panels, and they were good. They restructured that a few years ago. I liked the original model we had but ... you needed more staff and more time. Resources have been cut. Panels have been cut. So, we had four locality panels and I think that's now been split into two, and it is all down to funding, a lack of funding, so services get reduced because they haven't got the same manpower, people leave and then they don't replace.' (DSL, secondary, Northern Unitary)

Schools in Middle County also commented that local authority early help officers had previously attended TAC meetings to offer guidance and administrative support, but that this now occurred much less frequently.

While many of the schools we visited in four of the five local authorities had become increasingly sceptical about the value of completing a CAF or an EHA, this was not the case in Northern City. All but one of the schools we visited there reported using the new local authority EHA routinely to try to access early help services and to provide a framework for the multi-agency work they were leading. Crucially, schools could access guidance from social work consultants attached to one of three local early help hubs, and it was also reported that early help workers would attend TAC meetings. Furthermore, schools were also able to buy support from a dedicated family support service whose workers would often take the lead on managing the EHA.[1] Further details on how this worked are included in the following sections of this chapter.

Taking the lead

This section examines the experiences of school staff who had taken on the lead professional role at the early help level. Frequently school staff felt compelled to lead now that other agencies were less engaged in multi-agency working at this level. While many staff spoke positively about taking the lead and building on their relationships with children and families, unsurprisingly there were references from across all the authorities and across the MAT that schools were being asked to compensate for overstretched children's social care services.

'It seems to always fall on schools'

The lead professional role involves taking responsibility for the coordination of support provided to families by multiple agencies. It invariably requires a substantial time commitment, even more so when local authority early help officers are not on hand to offer guidance. Staff in schools sometimes felt pressured to take on the role because other agencies would not or could not commit sufficient resources. However, the main complaint was not about the time commitment or the administrative burden, it was that other agencies did not always engage even after schools agreed to lead. And as one head teacher explained, who was by no means alone in holding this view, this seemed to have become worse over recent years:

> 'Early help was meant to be a multi-agency approach ... but actually I'd say seven out of the ten early helps that I've got, they're not multi-agency, it's just me and mum and dad, or me and mum and nan. It's not a multi-agency approach because the school nurse can't come, health visitor can't come, it's because of their capacity and their workloads. ... Outside agencies don't come to meetings, so it's not what early help should be from my experiences in the past where we had every agency round the table.' (Head teacher, primary, Middle County)

Even though EHAs were in wider use in Northern City compared with other areas, schools here expressed similar complaints. There was a widely held view that getting the school 'to open an EHA' had become the default response in cases deemed not to meet the threshold for children's social care. This happened even when the welfare concerns that needed to be addressed appeared to be well outside the school's sphere of expertise or influence. The SENCo at one primary school commented:

> 'I do feel like schools are put at the front of it all to lead the [EHA], and sometimes you're sitting there thinking ... this is about housing, this is about other issues that's out of my control. I don't know what I'm writing about or doing ... so sometimes I do feel like education, it is just, well, they're in school, we'll be able to meet in school. I'm not saying schools are not going to be able to host them, but we

might not have the skills or the knowledge to know where to go to support the parent with the mental health issue or the housing issue, so I do feel like sometimes that's really, really hard.' (SENCo, primary, Northern City)

A secondary school DSL explained that they used to have more pupils on child protection and child in need plans, commenting:

'Since we've had the [EHAs] introduced, that's changed a lot ... you phone up and they say, right, stop there, before we go any further, is this child at risk of significant harm? And we might think they might well be, but at this point in time they're not because they're in front of us and they're safe in school. So, they might say, right, do an [EHA], and that seems to be the answer to a lot of the issues now.' (Deputy DSL, secondary, academy, Northern City)

The view that schools were effectively being asked to take the pressure off children's social care by managing cases at the early help level was expressed by schools across all the case study areas, as the following two quotes illustrate:

'What's tended to happen is that with the shrinkage of preventative, longer-term family work, family-focused social work, [and] the increasing ... [number of] children in need as opposed to child protection plans ... we will be the lead professional, which basically means it's up to us. ... The number of occasions when the teachers are lead professionals [has grown], definitely.' (Family support worker, secondary, academy, Rural Unitary)

'I'm not saying it's not part of our job, but our job has changed dramatically. We're becoming almost like family support workers or social workers because these cases are not being picked up.' (Student support manager, primary, academy, MAT)

Furthermore, even in cases where children's social care were involved, concerns were also expressed about social workers attempting to delegate work which schools did not feel comfortable or competent to handle, as in this instance:

'because they are stretched to [the] limit ... [they sometimes say] you as the school can lead it, but it's not for us to lead on this on. You're a social worker, you're involved, you need to lead it, it's not for us to lead ... we've had instances where [social workers] are working with a child, but they've got a concern about a parent's mental health. [They say] well, you can lead that … well actually no, because we don't see this, we are not in the home, we are not doing these visits, so I can't comment on Mum's mental health.' (Head of lower school, primary, Northern Unitary)

It is important to recognise that parental engagement at the early help level is voluntary. Getting some parents to engage, or keeping them engaged, could be problematic. These two quotes capture the frustration expressed:

'So, if they're [parents] not turning up, and we can't force them to turn up, then we have to hope that it meets the threshold for a referral somewhere; quite often it doesn't.' (Assistant head/deputy DSL, primary, London Borough)

'The threshold seems so high at the moment and everything's just getting passed down to an [EHA] … this Mum … she's quite within her rights to say to me – "do you know, I've decided I don't want this [EHA] any longer" – and then this family are just left … there's a massive, massive gap there.' (Home–school liaison worker, primary, Northern City)

In such cases it was argued that the involvement of children's social care, and the threat that cases could be escalated, was necessary. Similarly, schools wanted children's social care to continue some level of involvement where cases were 'stepped down' from child protection or child in need plans for schools to manage at the early help level.

Early help can work

Clearly the recent experiences of many schools, across all the case study areas, had been frustrating. However, in each area some school staff spoke more positively about early help and the role that schools played in bringing agencies together. For example, even though some schools in London Borough said that they had stopped using the CAF, the following DSL thought that this framework was still useful: "I think it's better that you have other agencies and other people, and you're also … you've got your timescales and your timelines … you have to do this by this date, so I think it's a lot tighter now, which is better" (DSL, primary, Northern City). Similarly, while some schools in Rural Unitary had also stopped using the CAF because they did not think it helped them to access support from other agencies, this person continued to see the value in bringing agencies together in a formal manner:

'I think if we're all sat there, everyone has to be very open and honest … [parents] say that to that person and that to that person and you don't really know what's going on. You spend a lot of time ... trying to find out actually what's happening, getting to the bottom of things. But the team around the child meetings mean that everyone's working towards the same goal, there's nowhere to hide, family support workers have been into the home, we're saying what we're seeing at school and it tends to work.' (Inclusion lead, primary, Rural Unitary)

In Northern City, despite some of the less-than-positive comments recorded earlier, schools were more engaged compared with elsewhere and most schools spoke positively about early help arrangements. It seems likely that this is the result of attempts by the local authority to simplify the relevant administrative processes combined with the growing expertise of school staff in using EHAs, as well as the availability of support from staff in the three early help hubs and the option to buy the support of a dedicated family support worker.

So, while there were concerns about cuts to services and the workload that attached to the role of lead professional, some schools recognised that they were in an ideal position to lead and that they were getting better at doing so, as the following two quotes illustrate:

'some [EHAs] are done so well that they have a real impact, and I think that's changed over the last few years. I think schools are getting much better ... at them, there's a real outcome.' (SENCo, secondary, academy, Northern City)

'I think schools more and more realise ... that children spend more time with us than any other professional, so we're probably the best ... organisation [to] manage the CAF or the [EHA], and I don't think schools are opposed to doing that.' (Head teacher, special school, Northern City)

Schools in Northern City were using EHAs far more frequently than elsewhere, where schools often looked to address concerns outside of the early help framework established by the local authority. However, across all the areas and the MAT it was clear that the willingness of schools to take on the lead role in managing early help was linked to the availability of pastoral and/or non-teaching staff. In primary schools at least, they were usually in contact with parents and other family members on a regular basis and were in a better position to build closer relationships with those families who needed support compared with colleagues and those from other agencies. One school-based family intervention worker, working in a special school, who had previously worked in public health, explained:

'Actually, to me, it makes sense here that I am lead professional. In my previous role, it didn't make sense for me to be lead professional because

I wasn't seeing the family frequently enough and I wasn't seeing the child frequently enough. However, here, we do see the child every day. ... But I know in previous roles, when it got discussed that it was going to [EHA] ... everybody would put their head down, nobody wanted to take that role on because it is so very, very time consuming.' (Family intervention worker, special school, Northern Unitary)

The level of pastoral support offered to children and families at all five of the special schools we visited, each in a different case study area, was particularly striking. In part this may be explained by an awareness of the pressures that go with bringing up children with special needs. This was amplified where parents had limited financial resources and/or had their own additional physical and/or mental health needs.

It was reported earlier that some schools highlighted difficulties in engaging with parents under voluntary early help arrangements and that it was felt that social worker involvement was needed in such cases. However, many schools, including most of those we visited in Northern City, spoke about the strength of relationships between schools and parents and identified this as arguably the key contributing factor to the provision of effective early help. Parents were said to often trust the advice given by staff in schools even if they were suspicious of other agencies, especially children's social care. Staff in the schools serving ethnically diverse populations had developed a good understanding of different cultural norms and attitudes and were often relied upon by other agencies to help communicate with non-English speakers. One head teacher in Northern City commented:

'Sometimes parents might not want other agencies involved. ... We have very good relationships with our parents ... particularly [DSL] has very good relationships, and I think parents see that she's there, whatever she's doing it's because she's caring, but also she has a role to play and it's about the child. ... We're not here to sit in judgement with our parents, we're here because ... we've got a concern or a concern has been raised, we need to see what we need to do about that. So, I think it's hugely helped because [we've] got a great foundation to build upon.' (Head teacher, primary, Northern City)

Schools as the providers and commissioners of welfare services

This section examines evidence relating to the welfare support provided or commissioned by schools outside of formal early help arrangements. The historic role played by schools as both education and welfare providers was highlighted in Chapter 2. However, research by Body (2020) suggests that, in the context of austerity, schools have been under pressure to raise additional resources or draw on their allocated budgets to provide or commission services themselves to respond to welfare concerns. The evidence presented here echoes these findings.

Family support

Making sure that children were well fed, clean and adequately clothed were some of the simplest but most important ways in which schools supported children and families. Schools serving the poorest communities often provided breakfast clubs and food vouchers or hampers for children and families facing financial hardship. Some schools also provided and laundered clothes. Moreover, it was apparent that many schools, particularly those in London Borough and Northern City, were providing more support than ever before. The introduction of Universal Credit, under which families received social security benefit payments only once a month instead of weekly, was highlighted by schools in these areas as a particular factor contributing to increased hardship. Schools were also supporting destitute families with no recourse to public funds, such as those with temporary immigration status. The vital role that some schools played in helping to meet children's most basic needs was highlighted by one pastoral worker in Northern City:

'Before I started working in a school, I never ever realised how much school meant to some children. It can mean everything to them. It's where they get their emotional needs met, it's where they get something to eat, it's where they get the majority of the support from.' (Home–school liaison worker, primary, Northern City)

Schools also relied on parents to help raise funds as well as local charities such as food banks to help meet basic needs. But school staff also made financial contributions themselves, as highlighted by one head teacher in London Borough:

'I'll be honest, I don't have any statistics on it, so it's not scientific, but I've been teaching in [London Borough] for 25 years and it's only in the last five or six years that we've had to … have staff collections and we give food to parents, we give out food vouchers. It wasn't something we did when I started teaching; [it] wasn't necessary, and it's increasingly so now.' (Head teacher/DSL, primary, London Borough)

However, schools provided much more than just food and clothing for children and families. Many parents rely on schools for basic information about how to access local services such as doctors, health centres, dentists and opticians. Families who were struggling to access benefits and housing sometimes asked staff to help with applications and act as their advocates. School staff even spoke about providing financial advice to struggling families. Generally, this kind of support was provided by non-teaching support staff, particularly in primary schools serving the poorest communities where it was more common to find staff employed as 'family support' or 'home–school liaison' workers. Discussing the importance of such roles in schools, the student support manager at one primary academy commented:

> 'I think it's really key that there are non-teaching pastoral members of staff within a school because ... without people like me, I can't see how schools in an area like this would be able ... to cope with all of the additional things that are now put back on a school. It wouldn't happen, would it?' (Student support manager, primary, academy, MAT)

Several secondary schools described how they brought pastoral staff, including 'heads of house' or 'heads of year', together from across the school in 'internal TACs' to make sure that information about children and families was shared and that everybody was working towards the same goals.

Pastoral staff also spoke about making direct referrals, or supporting parents to refer themselves, to agencies outside the early help arrangements that were in place, such as domestic violence support agencies and drug and alcohol services, as well as to parenting courses. More experienced staff were able to draw on their knowledge and experience of working with a whole range of public and voluntary agencies when making such referrals. However, for less experienced staff, or staff new to a local area, working outside of early help arrangements in this way was far more daunting. One deputy head, who had recently joined one of the MAT primary schools, explained that most of the school's EHAs were getting knocked back by the local authority and that she felt uncertain about which agencies to turn to for support. She would search the website for suggestions and while acknowledging a local family service was very good, she was not really sure what it could offer:

> 'they're at a meeting that I'm at later. It'll be really interesting to know what else they can offer us for these families that we're finding in difficulty. It may be that I'm not doing the right thing to tap into them, but I don't know that at the moment, because I'm [only] six months into it.' (Deputy head/DSL, primary, academy, MAT)

Mental health

Alongside poverty and neglect, the other area that schools felt most under pressure to address was the mental health of children and young people.

This was a major concern in all the secondary schools we visited, but also for many primary schools. In each local area schools highlighted how difficult it was to access support for the most serious cases through CAMHS. Moreover, the mental health of pupils was a shared concern across schools in this study, from those serving the poorest communities to the most affluent. Both secondary and primary school staff made a connection between rising levels of poor mental health and the use of social media. Secondary school staff were particularly concerned about the mental health of female students and specifically about the rising number of incidents of self-harm. Within primary schools it was generally children who had suffered a bereavement or had parents who had separated who concerned staff most.

It is important to recognise that this research was undertaken before any new national initiatives associated with the government Green Paper *Transforming Children and Young People's Mental Health Provision* (Department of Health and Department for Education, 2017) had been implemented. Nevertheless, over half of the schools visited across the case study areas reported that they already paid for some form of mental health provision. Some schools employed their own counsellor or therapist, while others paid for dedicated time from an educational psychologist, separate from any provision available through the local authority. In Northern Unitary a local charity had previously provided schools with free access to counselling services. As a result of cuts to their grant income, they had to introduce a charge but six of the 10 schools we visited were paying to continue to access this support. In Rural Unitary schools also had the option to buy in additional support from a local service designed to respond to moderate mental health concerns below the threshold for CAMHS.

However, Rural Unitary was an exception as far as the support of local authority or NHS support was concerned. In other areas schools were more likely to be left to determine their own arrangements. In some instances what was described as 'low-level mental health support' or similar was provided by staff in schools where they had attended training courses such as mental health 'first aid'. But there was some uncertainty about how effective school-based mental health support alone could be:

'So for me, I've done youth mental health first aid training, so again I'm not a specialist, I'm a pastoral worker in school. So you do the training and you're just supporting these kids the best that you can with the resources that are out there, really ... You kind of feel like you're going out into the deep dark waters, what if you make a mistake, actually, what if you do the wrong thing, what if you say the wrong thing? I know you probably won't because of the nature of your role and your training, but it's a worry.' (Family liaison officer, primary, Northern Unitary)

Pressure on budgets

It is evident that many schools go to extraordinary lengths to both educate and promote the welfare of children and young people. However, it is apparent that the challenges they have faced in this regard over recent years have been at least in part a consequence of increased hardships experienced by some families and communities. Significantly, this has placed increasing strain on schools' own resources at a time when funding per pupil has been falling (Farquharson et al, 2021), as highlighted in Chapter 1. This has left school leaders facing a difficult dilemma about whether to prioritise continued investment in pastoral support or in teaching roles. The DSL in one primary school explained why they could not offer more in terms of family support:

> 'We are trying to do lots of things with the children, but we haven't got the finances to employ someone from school to work with [families] … that's what the family support service does. But we can't buy into that service now because we can't afford it. … And the educational psychologist … we buy in so much, but we could do with it every week, but we can't … we [only] have so much time every quarter.' (DSL, primary, Northern City)

At another primary school the head teacher described the difficult choice that some schools faced in terms of prioritising resources for teaching and learning versus pastoral support:

> 'It's like, do I not meet the needs, the safeguarding needs, or do I not meet the educational needs of some of the children? … so the funding is huge to this, and I know a lot of schools have had to reduce their pastoral teams because you need people in the classrooms to teach, and they're not classroom based, but they just do such a vital element of the work of the school that it's really difficult, really difficult.' (Head teacher, primary, Northern Unitary)

At this school the decision had been taken to cut the number of classroom-based teaching assistant posts to protect the pastoral team.

Concluding comments

We reported in the previous chapter that many schools referring cases to children's social care thought that thresholds had risen and that they were increasingly being advised to consider how families could be supported under local early help arrangements instead. This chapter has examined the evidence our research uncovered about schools' experiences of multi-agency working at this level, with a particular focus on poverty, neglect and mental health problems. It was clear that cuts to funding had made it more difficult for schools to access support from external agencies in each of the case study areas. Some agencies had disappeared, while others were now operating at reduced capacity and with long waiting lists. In this context, some schools were reluctant to open a CAF or an EHA because this involved significant work without the promise of additional support for families. In some areas schools also reported that support provided by local authority early help officers to deal with administrative requirements had also diminished. Furthermore, school staff who had taken on the lead professional role commonly complained that other agencies were not fully engaged and that they often felt left to deal with a range of child and family welfare concerns outside of their area of expertise or sphere of influence. These included trying to engage with parents to address safeguarding concerns where children's social care was increasingly asking schools to take responsibility, possibly in an attempt to manage the demands on their resources.

A government-sponsored review of the mental health and well-being policies of 100 schools (Brown, 2018) inferred that 'schools were identifying pupils' additional emotional and psychological needs by the extent of their disruptive behaviour' (p 25) and concluded that schools needed to shift to focus on mental health and well-being, confirming that this area is likely to devolve further to schools' responsibilities in future. The Green Paper *Transforming Children and Young People's Mental Health Provision* (Department of Health and Department for Education, 2017) had set out the government's approach to addressing the deficits in mental health support for children and young people. As well as piloting a four-week waiting time standard for CAMHS, government emphasised the central role of schools in this area by promising more 'talking therapies' and more lessons in mental health. It also proposed that all schools should have a designated senior lead for mental health, who would oversee the school's approach to mental health and well-being. They would work with newly created Mental Health Support Teams that would be based in schools, with a focus on providing both early intervention and a wider range of support to staff and parents. Where they have been established these teams have continued to work virtually through the pandemic, but their planned expansion has been delayed. It also remains to be seen if schools have the capacity to respond.

However, notwithstanding the challenges and frustrations that were encountered, the evidence reviewed here has also demonstrated that schools across all case study areas were committing their own resources to provide family support and respond to mental health concerns. The employment of support staff was fundamental in this regard. This has required school leaders to make difficult choices about how best to meet both their teaching and broader welfare responsibilities. Our research has also underlined the importance of ensuring that schools have access to adequate guidance and support to make sure that pastoral services can be delivered effectively. Access to advice and support through early help hubs and the option to buy family support workers from the local authority was a key feature of the wider engagement with EHAs in Northern City compared with elsewhere. Similarly, schools in Rural Unitary benefitted from access to support for dealing with mental health concerns that fell below the CAMHS threshold. The absence of support elsewhere left some staff feeling daunted and uneasy at times about how best to support children and families.

Reflections on the case studies reported in Chapters 4–6

Alun Rees, Alun Rees Learning Limited and Consultant to the Rees Centre for the Study of Fostering and Education, University of Oxford

Ever since *Every Child Matters* schools in general, and head teachers in particular, have been concerned by the number of times their staff have been nominated as lead professionals. It is clear this has not changed. It isn't a surprise, though, given that schools see children more than any other service and have more routine contact with families than any other service. Few public services are as trusted by their communities as schools. They are *the* universal service in this context; and for all the frustrations and concerns about stress and workload it is clear that school staff recognise that in a way they perhaps didn't at the birth of ECM.

What has changed is that with ECM came a range of local authority targeted services upon which lead professionals could draw. It was disheartening to read how many times a school-based lead professional was scratching around for the support they needed to make a difference to a child or family. Too often in these chapters school staff report that they don't feel it's worth taking the time to complete a CAF, or even a more streamlined local alternative, as that investment too rarely delivers the support being sought. This is corrosive of both DSL team morale and self-belief; the very things that effective safeguarding requires. If they feel they are all that's standing between a child and the future risk of harm then their stress rises and emotional and professional burnout beckons.

Perhaps the most distressing observation made in the study was of a case moving from referral to care very swiftly when the school felt that an earlier response to concerns could have kept a child at home. Despite efforts to make thresholds, explicit documents describing them are, inevitably, loosely phrased. They must be to accommodate professional judgement, and that requires trust among partners. Social care may consider that schools make too many (and poorly timed) referrals, and schools complain that social workers do not trust their judgement. 'Twas ever thus, but perhaps the opportunities to break down those barriers of distrust are rarer than they used to be. Social workers have never had such high and complex caseloads while the demand schools face has grown to include radicalisation, child exploitation and emotional well-being, alongside neglect and abuse. The opportunities for local DSL networks and frontline children's social care managers to come together and talk about the issues are too rare. Too often their first contact is a disagreement about a referral; that is no way to build the relationship trust requires. Relationships take time and time costs money: an all too rare commodity. Perhaps the reported availability of safeguarding networks offers a cost-effective way to develop face-to-face relationships between schools and social care.

All this adds up to schools being asked to hold more, and in their view riskier, cases. Growing levels of disadvantage are generating more concerns at a time when the targeted services safety net schools could rely on has been largely dismantled due to government funding cuts. Schools have been commissioners for some time, but it was very concerning that even when they tried to, the range of charities and other providers was also thinner than it was. The sense of isolation some DSLs felt was very real; the fear of getting something wrong or that there was something they could have done better. It made a strong case for professional supervision that went beyond the head teacher's open door; and whose door is open for the head when they are the DSL?

To end more positively, though, this study shows, in comparison to 2007 when these issues were explored by one of the authors, that almost all school staff now take for granted the view that safeguarding is the responsibility of all of them. It was, frankly, a relief to find very few 'I'm a teacher not a social worker' responses. It was encouraging to instead find most of the responders took the view that 'we're all children's workers, now, and they'll learn better if we get it right'. What shines through the responses of school staff is the moral purpose to do all they can for the families they serve. That, though, is no excuse for central government to take advantage of them. The underfunding of local authority services has placed much greater burdens on schools and seems to work on the premise that schools will continue to just fill the gap; a gap that has certainly grown during the pandemic.

While schools are doing all they can they have neither the range of expertise nor the range of interventions at their disposal that are necessary to meet the needs they are identifying. There are creative approaches on view here in both schools and local authorities in relation to recruitment decisions and both process and structure choices. However, the risk is that all government will do is look at 'Northern City' or 'London Borough' or somewhere else and conclude that negligible additional resource is necessary to spread and scale models. They have greater responsibilities than that and should fulfil them.

PART III

Concluding thoughts

7

Schools and safeguarding: aligning expectations with reality

Introduction

As the recognition of the nature and prevalence of child abuse and neglect has increased so has recognition of the need for agencies and professionals to work together to respond effectively (Horwath and Morrison, 2011). This book has charted how schools have long contributed to both the well-being and protection of children, and how they have been gradually drawn into a wider network of professionals and agencies with a shared ambition. They have engaged with the vision of a 'continuum' of services from parenting support and early help to compulsory intervention (Laming, 2003). The ECM (HM Government, 2003) agenda represented a shift towards a family support model. Even though ECM was short lived, as were many of the structures that accompanied it, it heralded a sea change in the way agencies accepted greater responsibility for this work.

Since then, however, to use the 'pendulum' analogy, policy has once more veered away from an emphasis on support and towards child protection interventions. The death of Peter Connelly in 2008 and the change of government in 2010 both influenced this change of direction. Despite the recommendations contained in Professor Munro's 2011 review of child protection, which the government had commissioned and which recommended that local authorities should be legally required to provide early intervention services to families, the following year the Secretary of State for Education, Michael Gove (2012), made a particularly bullish speech at an NSPCC event. In it he signalled an approach based on rescuing children at risk of neglect or abuse from 'a life of soiled nappies and scummy baths, chaos and hunger, hopelessness and despair', rather than supporting parents to be in a better position to care for them. This attitude did little to stem the rate of referrals to children's social care, which rose by 22 per cent between 2008 and 2018 (Association of Directors of Children's Services (ADCS), 2018).

It is impossible to divorce the research reported in this book from the context of 2017–19, when it was conducted. The austerity measures that were put in place in 2010 were having a major impact on local authorities. The National Audit Office (2018b) reported that local authorities' central government funding fell by an estimated 49.1 per cent in real terms between 2010 and 2017, equating to a 28.6 per cent real-terms reduction in 'spending power'. Hastings et al (2017) found that the cuts were having a disproportionate impact on the most deprived areas. The Local Government Association (LGA) (2019) and the ADCS (Dickinson, 2019) examined the impact of this on children's social care, concluding that services have been placed under significant strain. In its evidence to the House of Commons Housing, Communities and Local Government Select Committee (2019, p 9) the LGA said 'local authority spending on children's social care has risen, [but] it has not kept pace with growing demand [leaving councils having] to make difficult decisions about the allocation of scarce resources'. This increase in spend was driven by large increases in the number of children and young people receiving statutory child protection support, leading to the closure of non-statutory services such as many children's centres and early help provision to allow local authorities to support those services they were legally required to provide. As a result, the ADCS (2018) suggested that the surviving early help services were holding more complex cases in response to increased pressure on statutory services.

Reviewing the research

Our research contributes to a better understanding of the effect of these measures and the context of austerity on the role of schools in relation to child protection and safeguarding and on the wider multi-agency context. In Chapter 1 we set out the two questions which the research sought to address. In the first place we wanted to know how effectively the multi-agency arrangements at local government level supported schools in the identification, referral and management of child protection and safeguarding concerns. We adopted a wide definition of multi-agency working to cover all interactions between agencies that were covered in the research and in this book. In the second, we sought to understand how staff in schools made decisions in relation to child protection concerns and the support they received to do so. This also allowed us to identify any differences that could be linked to their relationship with their local authorities. The research allowed us to explore and answer these two questions as well as to uncover how local authorities approach their statutory and non-statutory safeguarding obligations.

While they are so much more, it is possible to view schools as small units working with agencies that have more 'corporate' identities, whether they are children's social care or the various agencies under the umbrella of the NHS. Until relatively recently all state-maintained schools were part of their local authorities, even though they have always been, to some extent, semi-autonomous and identified by their ethos, sector, leadership and the population they serve. This autonomy was extended by the Education

Reform Act of 1988, which introduced 'local management of schools', meaning that many of the functions that were previously the domain of local authorities were delegated to schools. However, apart from the short-lived grant-maintained schools initiative,[1] which meant a small proportion of schools were funded directly by a grant from central government, schools remained the responsibility of the local authority. As discussed in Chapter 2, publicly funded schools independent of local authorities re-emerged in 2002 under a Labour government policy to target poorly performing schools, but it was under the Conservative-Liberal Democrat Coalition Government that came to office in 2010 that the transition accelerated. Local authorities have overarching statutory responsibility for safeguarding and promoting the welfare of all children and young people in their area and this means that local authorities retain the duty to oversee child protection and safeguarding in maintained schools and academies, as well as schools in the independent sector. In their report *Safeguarding Children Across Services: Messages from Research*, Davies and Ward (2012) predicted the challenges arising from the increasingly fragmented educational estate, but before our study no one had explored the effect that the greater autonomy from local authority control enjoyed by academies has on the safeguarding practice of such schools or on their wider engagement in inter-agency safeguarding arrangements.

Multi-agency arrangements and schools

Our scoping interviews had drawn attention to some negative aspects of academisation, as well as to the increased level of school autonomy in general, which threatened and even reduced the capacity of some local authorities to monitor and support safeguarding and child protection arrangements in schools. There were concerns that too many schools, whatever their designation, prioritised their examination results over the welfare of some pupils, particularly in relation to exclusions and off-rolling – when a student/pupil is removed from a school without a formal permanent exclusion, often by encouraging a family to home-educate a child to avoid an exclusion. This was tied into the limited powers local authorities had to safeguard children who were in alternative settings.

These case studies confirmed schools as one of the key agencies with regard to child protection and safeguarding in all local areas. The importance of schools' continued strategic involvement at the local level under new multi-agency safeguarding arrangements – in which schools are 'relevant agencies' but not one of the 'safeguarding partners' – was emphasised by schools and other agencies. We also found that academies were no less engaged in multi-agency working than local authority-maintained schools. A far more defining factor than academisation was the context in which the schools operated, for example levels of poverty in the local community or where a local authority adopted an inclusive approach to all schools, irrespective of type. While there were differences in the nature and extent to which schools engaged with children's social care and other agencies, this engagement was primarily shaped by the level and type of need across the school community and the availability of support services. Most schools, regardless of designation, spoke positively about the training provided by the local authority and the support received from the education safeguarding advisory teams. In general, they also welcomed the establishment of Multi-Agency Safeguarding Hub (MASH) and were content with the responses they received to the most serious cases. However, while they valued being able to access informal advice before deciding to refer, there was a tension between the MASH providing a consultation service and its role as a screening system. This was, perhaps, associated with more general tensions expressed by schools around some referrals. In both the scoping interviews and surveys, staff working in children's social care had been more certain that schools were content with the responses they received when they made referrals than those in LSCBs and education safeguarding teams. The views of schools in this study were closer to the latter than to those in children's social care.

Most schools thought that the thresholds around children's social care interventions were too high and that they had risen over the previous five to 10 years. Threshold documents reflect the continuum of help and support, as well as providing information on levels of need and indicators that a child or young person may need additional support. While there was a reasonably high awareness of these documents, particularly in secondary schools, there was not a great deal of confidence in how they were applied. Along this continuum, services become increasingly targeted and specialised according to the level of need. When schools were not able to match an observed level of need with the response received, their trust in threshold documents was undermined. They understood, and were committed to, the argument that providing early help is far more effective in promoting the welfare of children – and keeping them safe – than reacting later when problems arise. There were many examples of schools' engagement in school- and community-based early help interventions, as well as examples of already stretched budgets being used to commission support externally. However, schools were frustrated when screening by children's social care led to cases being referred back to them to manage without additional support or guidance, especially when they saw what had been early help services being deployed to cases of high need and even to cases where child protection plans were in place. As far as schools were concerned, this left them to manage cases of increasing complexity, including those they considered should be handled by children's social care.

Within this context it is important that the multi-agency arrangements at local government level support schools to fulfil their role in relation to child protection and safeguarding. To measure the 'congruence' – that is the alignment of views – within local authorities, we compared how closely aligned the strategic views were of staff in education, children's social care, and LSCBs. Using this as a basis for investigation we found no strong evidence that 'congruence' between the agencies working with schools had any consistent impact on the quality or effectiveness of the support provided to schools. But it is important to note that this measure of 'congruence' is only one aspect of an incredibly complex kaleidoscope of relationships between agencies and, perhaps more importantly, people.

School staff accepted that they were required to work with other agencies and, as far as the schools in this study were concerned, it was a duty that had been absorbed into their systems and practice, but it also depended on relationships that had developed between agencies and individuals. Horwath and Morrison (2007) found that professional cultures and organisational structures could get in the way, and that determination, as well as time and trust, were required to succeed. Time can be at a premium, particularly considering the pressures on staff working in schools and children's social care, as well as in the other agency with which schools were anxious to work, CAMHS. Trust is also a fundamental component of multi-agency working, yet such trust was easily undermined where the high turnover of social workers could create instability for families and professionals, as well as a negative perception of the whole profession.

Engagement and decision making in schools

Overall the arrangements in schools looked very different from those in place when a similar study was undertaken around 15 years earlier (reported in Baginsky, 2007). The subject of that study had been schools and their interactions with what was then social services over child protection, whereas the recent one also considered safeguarding. In the earlier study many designated leads for child protection lacked confidence and understanding around thresholds, which contributed to their bemusement over some decisions that were taken. The majority of DSLs in the case study schools reported in this book thought they did have a reasonable understanding of thresholds, but they often did not have the opportunity to challenge, or even discuss, decisions which they believed were not in children's best interest.

Compared with the earlier study there was substantially more training for all staff working in schools. Although face-to-face training was usually the preferred option, the introduction of online training provided an element of flexibility to enable staff to access training on specific topics or if they had missed a face-to-face session. This had supported the ethos of safeguarding being 'everybody's business' that had emerged in Lord Laming's inquiry into the death of Victoria Climbié (2003) and was frequently voiced in interviews with school staff, where it was certainly not a mere mantra. On the whole DSLs were more experienced than those interviewed in the previous study, and the majority now had deputies and sometimes even safeguarding teams.

Many schools, including most secondary schools, had implemented electronic management information systems to manage large volumes of data recorded by staff regarding safeguarding and wider welfare concerns. The guidance provided by the various iterations of *Working Together to Safeguard Children* and *Keeping Children Safe in Education*, the statutory responsibilities set out in the Children Act 2004 and the inclusion of safeguarding as a major focus in Ofsted inspections, have all contributed to an improved understanding and engagement in this work. The demands, challenges and uncertainties that accompanied this activity meant that most schools – whether local authority maintained or academies – worked closely with the local education safeguarding advisers and, where possible, engaged with those in other schools doing similar work.

Despite schools' commitment there were substantial pressures that accompanied their statutory responsibilities. Even the most experienced and well-trained DSLs explained that safeguarding work, often involving the management of difficult relationships with parents, could be time consuming and emotionally draining. Schools were under pressure to respond to rising levels of need, often linked to poverty and/or poor mental health, at a time when external services were harder to access. One of the most challenging scenarios for schools was the cumulative effect of long-term neglect because, while it was evident over time, unless there was a significant event, more serious than any other that preceded it, children's social care did not intervene, even though neglect and other forms of abuse frequently coexist. Similarly, schools were also under pressure to provide support to children and young people with low or moderate level mental health needs that did not meet the threshold for CAMHS. They were also dealing with concerns emerging from dangers that were still relatively new to them, particularly online safety, the Prevent agenda, and child criminal exploitation.

When local authority early help support was absent, or considered to be insufficient, school staff often felt unprepared to deal with the extent of the needs of children and families, but the majority attempted to do something. It is important to remember that these demands were being made alongside both the increasing demands made on schools to demonstrate academic progress and attainment by pupils, and questions about the financial sustainability when budgets had been falling, in real terms, from 2015 onwards (Sibieta, 2020). The commitment of schools was reflected in the resources many allocated to safeguarding work, including the employment of support staff. Some had also commissioned services directly when support under multi-agency early help arrangements had been lacking, although some local authority staff also expressed concern regarding the lack of any quality assurance of the services schools were accessing. So, while school staff have to a large extent accepted greater engagement in safeguarding and child protection, as the professionals with the greatest level of contact with children and families, some experienced head teachers expressed concern that the demands upon them were becoming untenable.

Final thoughts

Some of the challenges exposed by this study are already being addressed in policy, including the urgent need for more mental health support for children and young people, although this represents a further example of responsibility being laid on schools for delivery of 'first aid' responses. Others are fairly readily addressed, including arguments for greater regulation to safeguard children who are not in registered or mainstream schools, particularly home-schooled children. But the widening gap between what schools feel able to contribute and the point at which children's social care accepts responsibility necessitates a holistic re-evaluation of the system, which the government's review of child protection announced in January 2021 may not be set up to address. The earlier study (Baginsky, 2007) quoted the title of a paper written by an eminent educational sociologist 'Schools Cannot Compensate for Society' (Bernstein, 1970). With hindsight it would have been fairer to say that schools cannot do this alone. Without a robust model of early help schools will continue to feel that they are dealing with needs that they do not have the skills or resources to manage and, in that respect, reflect the widespread views expressed by teachers in the earlier study, the fieldwork for which was conducted 20 years ago.

Previous governmental responses to problems of inter-agency communication or collaboration have generally been to legislate and/or reorganise. As a result, the legislation and guidance that are needed are in place and the study provides the evidence that these have led to improved engagement and role clarity, despite the frustrations that arose from different organisational practices between agencies. This improvement will be jeopardised if expectations exceed schools' capacity and capability to deliver and this, in turn, leads them to refocus and pull back from a wider welfare agenda. Although it was feared that the greater decentralisation of education would weaken the role of schools in a multi-agency approach to child protection and safeguarding, from the evidence collected during this study this does not appear to have been the case. A far greater threat is, however, emerging from the expectations placed on schools without the corresponding level of resourcing to meet these demands.

It was very evident that schools were concerned about being expected to work beyond their professional competence, especially when they felt they were left alone to cope when other agencies were overwhelmed or where services had either closed or were not available. While these concerns could represent a threat to schools' engagement in multi-agency working in general, and specifically in safeguarding and child protection, the schools in our study were still keen to work with other agencies even if they were sometimes frustrated by the reality, and possibly frustrating others. Writing about integrated teams, Rushmer and Pallis (2002) drew attention to the importance of merging the skills, experience and knowledge of different professionals to achieve the best outcome. They were also clear that it was counter-productive to blur professional boundaries. Their findings are just as relevant to multi-agency working.

It was evident from the survey reported in Chapter 3 and earlier research conducted by Baginsky and Holmes (2015) that LSCBs had played a key role in supporting agencies to work together, not least over training and auditing arrangements. It remains to be seen if arrangements made by the new Safeguarding Partnerships will be as successful. While it had not always proved easy to find the right arrangements to involve schools in LSCBs, particularly after the increase in the number of academies, progress was being made up the point when they were disbanded (Baginsky and Holmes, 2015). When schools were not made a statutory partner in the multi-agency partnership arrangements that replaced LSCBs, it was a backwards step, probably in terms of practice but most certainly in sending a message to schools that they were a 'second class' partner. There is equal, if not more, diversity and variation within Health but that did not stop it from becoming a statutory partner. Supporting families where problems are complex, persistent and often deep-seated is not something that one agency can address alone. Neither is multi-agency work easy. It is not only multidimensional, it can also mean different things to different individuals and groups. Milbourne (2005) pointed out it is also complicated by organisational and professional norms, as well as inspection and performance frameworks. She was writing at a time when multi-agency work was central to government policies, with structures and posts created to support its implementation. These developments were the subject of a considerable body of research, some of which is quoted in earlier chapters. It was not easy to translate the intentions into practice, as failures of communication between agencies so evident in Serious Case Reviews testify. It was, and continues to be, threatened by workforce churn, professional cultures, agency and service reorganisation, and a lack of resources. Alfandari (2019) examined multi-agency working in Israel and found the same barriers and facilitators as those reported in the US, Canada, Australia and the UK existed there, although she found that schools were the most active participant of all agencies in the multi-agency fora she studied.

Reflecting on our work with schools there are two elements which appeared to be missing. While there was a considerable amount of training in place, much of which was relevant to multi-agency working, there were no references to training that advanced partnership working to a level that enabled schools to work across professional boundaries. This was closely associated with the second element, that is, a commitment that not only supports schools to be better integrated into children's services provision, but one that is committed to full engagement of schools in both strategic and operational decision making. This will require a model of practice that fits local communities, rather than being imposed from the centre, and which involves stronger links with other professionals and promotes a much closer integration of services to make the systems stronger than the individuals in them. Consequently, the composition and experience of any group that makes decisions to intervene in a family's life – or not to do so – would be strengthened. In turn, this should make it more likely that the right decisions are taken for children and young people. This requires opportunities to bring people together and providing appropriate learning that allows each professional to understand their role in this arena and that of other agencies, within a space where they can debate decisions. COVID-19 has been a game changer. It seems certain that practice will not return to a pre-COVID norm. For example, remote working, which has mushroomed during the pandemic, looks set to become part of business as usual, but it would be a mistake to think that the old ways of doing things will transfer seamlessly. As the nature of work changes transformational thinking will be required to make sure that the structures that emerge are designed to address what did not work in the past. It was clear from our study that there is still an opportunity to draw schools more tightly into a truly multi-agency approach that would provide the opportunity to correct the often fragmented and asymmetric response to families. The pandemic might offer the opportunity to do so.

Postscript

In this postscript, we take the opportunity to reflect briefly on the ways in which schools' safeguarding work and their collaboration with other agencies were affected by COVID-19. This discussion draws on early research on the impact of the pandemic, including our own. It also covers several other areas where the role of schools had been highlighted in the years following the research. In the final section we briefly consider the implications for schools' future involvement in multi-agency working after the pandemic in the context of a range of ongoing or planned national reviews of various aspects of education and safeguarding policy.

As we were writing this book, we saw rapid developments in child safeguarding policy and practice as a result of the COVID-19 pandemic. In the preceding chapters we have documented the extent to which schools had been feeling increasing pressures in the decade prior to the pandemic as a consequence of rising poverty levels, reduced funding for child and family welfare services, and overstretched school budgets. Even before the pandemic many school leaders were facing difficult choices regarding how best to fulfil both their teaching and welfare responsibilities. Moreover, we showed how many schools, particularly those serving the poorest communities, felt compelled to take on additional responsibilities as the demands on children's social care grew and early help services were cut back.

The impact of the measures to combat the pandemic magnified many of the pre-existing challenges that schools and other agencies were facing. Poverty or financial instability and parental stress increased for many families, the availability of professional and voluntary support networks diminished, and disengagement with universal services was legitimised by government 'stay home' guidance. Under lockdown conditions more children were formally and informally categorised as 'vulnerable' and the fear was that children already known to services could be exposed to heightened risk (Children's Commissioner, 2020; Romanou and Belton, 2020; Child Safeguarding Review Panel, 2021). Identification of child protection concerns became more challenging, reflected in initial decreases in referrals to children's social care, and reports of increased complexity and severity of referrals (Baginsky and Manthorpe, 2020a; Driscoll et al, 2020; 2021; Pearce and Miller, 2020).

The first stage of Baginsky and Manthorpe's (2020a; 2020b; 2021) research involved case studies of responses to COVID-19 in 15 local authority children's social care departments. This was followed up with more in–depth research in five of these authorities and a short survey completed by 105 schools. Discussions with a range of professionals in each of the five areas focused specifically on the robustness of multi-agency working with schools during the first national lockdown. Driscoll et al's (2020; 2021) research included 67 interviews with lead safeguarding professionals from children's social care, Local Children's Safeguarding Partnerships, health, police, law, education and mental health services in 24 London boroughs carried out between June and September 2020. This was followed by a national survey of safeguarding professionals carried out between February and March 2021, which received 417 responses.

The impact of school closures on safeguarding practice

The implications of the closure of schools to most children were widely regarded as one of the most concerning of the measures adopted to combat the spread of the pandemic. Only the children of 'key workers' and those judged to be 'vulnerable' were able to continue to attend a school building. Other agencies with safeguarding responsibilities, including children's social care services, were able to adapt quickly to new patterns of home-based working and 'virtual' meetings (Baginsky and Manthorpe, 2020a). However, for school-based staff, continuing to meet their safeguarding responsibilities became much more difficult once most children switched to being educated or remaining at home. This section considers what the evidence collected in the research studies highlighted earlier tells us about (a) safeguarding arrangements for children who continued to attend school during the first lockdown; and (b) how schools worked to 'keep in touch' with children not attending school for whom they or partner agencies had concerns.

School places for 'vulnerable' children

During the first national lockdown in England, between March and June 2020, children categorised as 'vulnerable' were entitled, but not required, to continue to attend a school building alongside the children of 'key workers'. Central government guidance defined vulnerable children as including those in receipt of statutory services under the Children Act 1989; children with an Education, Health and Care (EHC) Plan whose needs could not be met safely in the home environment; and children otherwise assessed as vulnerable by educational providers or local authorities (DfE, 2020b). Additional places were also offered for children who did not fit this definition, but for whom schools or other agencies had welfare concerns. However, the criteria applied differed widely between local authorities and schools (Baginsky and Manthorpe, 2020b).

Nationally, the initial uptake of school places for vulnerable children during the first lockdown was very low. It was reported that only 5 per cent had continued to attend school (Simpson, 2020). Driscoll et al (2021) found that concerns relating to the health of children and their parents or carers were the most common reasons given for the non-attendance of vulnerable children. This may have been influenced by fears across the wider community as well as the government's clear 'stay at home' message. But Driscoll et al (2021) also reported that in some cases it was felt that children were happier or more secure at home and some refused to attend because the label of vulnerability was thought to be stigmatising. Local authorities and schools adopted a range of strategies to encourage attendance. The most common was for school DSLs, or other members of staff known to the family, to talk to parents and encourage them to allow their child or children to attend. School staff also responded to parental concerns regarding children's behaviour at home or disinterest in schoolwork by encouraging school attendance for children where they had concerns. Another approach was to work with professionals in other agencies, including children's social care, health, school improvement services or youth services, to develop coordinated multi-agency virtual contact with parents to encourage school attendance. Although the initial take-up of places for vulnerable children was low, it did increase over the course of the first lockdown (DfE, 2021c). However, persistent absence increased to 16.3 per cent in secondary schools in autumn 2020, compared with 15.0 per cent in 2019.

'Keeping in touch' with children not attending school

Schools also had to do their best to ensure the safety and well-being of children who remained at home during the lockdown. This included children officially categorised as vulnerable and others for whom schools and/ or other agencies had welfare concerns before the pandemic. Other children were considered to be newly at risk following the 'stay at home' guidance (Baginsky and Manthorpe, 2020b; 2021; Wilson and Waddell, 2020). The lockdown placed more families under financial pressure and heightened concerns related to poverty and neglect, and associated risks including exposure to domestic violence and substance misuse. Additional concerns were related to the social isolation and mental health of children and young people during extended periods at home. The Child Safeguarding Practice Review Panel (2021) examined data from Serious Incident Notifications, rapid reviews, Local Child Safeguarding Practice Reviews and Serious Case Reviews from 1 January to 31 December 2020. This analysis highlighted incidents of self-harm, exposure to sexual abuse and online bullying. Furthermore, the loss of support from friends, trusted adults and schools appeared to have impacted on children and young people's mental health in ways which were evidenced in all cases of suicide reviewed. At the same time there was a significant increase in pupils being removed from school to be home-educated, which showed a 34 per cent rise in the number of children being home-educated in 2020/21 compared with the previous year (Association of Directors of Children's Services, 2021).

The evidence presented in this book has shown how many schools go above and beyond what is required of them under official safeguarding guidance to support children and families facing the most difficult circumstances. This commitment was clearly evident during the pandemic. Informants in Driscoll et al's (2021) study highlighted the additional burden placed on schools. There were many examples reported in the national media of school staff delivering meals and working to close the 'digital divide' to ensure that children could access online learning. Importantly, these activities were also used by school staff as an opportunity check on children and families for whom they had concerns. These doorstep visits were carried out more frequently for children and families judged as higher risk, and examples of meetings in gardens and parks to check on the welfare of children were also highlighted by professionals (Baginsky and Manthorpe, 2020b; Driscoll et al, 2021). However, some of the schools surveyed by Baginsky and Manthorpe (2020b) felt that these visits were necessary because other agencies, including children's social care and health, became much less active in this regard during the lockdown. Some schools reported finding it more difficult to engage with children's social care and early help services during the lockdown and after children returned to school when new concerns started to emerge. It was felt that COVID-19 had impacted on the availability of suitably qualified and experienced staff and that agency or temporary staff drafted in were not always up to speed with local systems and processes (Baginsky and Manthorpe, 2020b).

However, it is only fair to point out that there were some teachers who said they found it easier to contact social workers as so many of them were working from home and some even provided their mobile phone numbers, which they had seemed reluctant to do previously. There was also evidence of other positive developments in multi-agency working during the first lockdown. The rapid and largely unproblematic shift to virtual meetings of professionals in most local authority areas was pivotal to maintaining inter-agency dialogue, and in many instances helped to improve the engagement of agencies such as health and the police, who had not always attended in-person meetings (Baginsky and Manthorpe, 2020a). In the five local authority areas investigated by Baginsky and Manthorpe (2020b) substantial plans were implemented to ensure regular and formal information sharing between schools, children's social care services and other agencies in relation to high-risk cases. Driscoll et al (2021) argued that the central role played by schools in keeping in touch with families was also important in so far as it helped families to feel supported rather than threatened during the lockdown. This finding is consistent with the evidence presented in this book regarding the more positive relationships schools very often have with families facing difficulties compared to children's social care services and other agencies.

The new multi-agency working arrangements put in place during the pandemic were not always suitable or effective. Baginsky and Manthorpe (2020a; 2020b) and Driscoll et al (2021) highlighted concerns regarding the engagement of parents in virtual multi-agency safeguarding meetings, sometimes because they lacked the technology or skills to be able to engage. Driscoll et al (2021) also found that some parents were unresponsive to school-led approaches to keeping in touch and that children's social care services, and in some cases the police, had to be called upon to follow up. This is consistent with findings reported in this book regarding the difficulty school staff sometimes had in engaging parents in voluntary early help or child in need arrangements. Some professionals advocated a different approach where there were safeguarding concerns. Most of the professionals surveyed by Driscoll et al (2021) thought that school attendance should have been mandatory for children with low clinical risks associated with COVID-19. Given the pressures on school staffing levels due to infection and shielding arrangements, it is difficult to see how this could have been sustained at the height of the lockdowns. However, although one local authority in north-west England reported making school attendance a condition of child in need and child protection plans, interview attendees at the end of project Policy Lab expressed ethical misgivings about such schemes, given that family members might be medically vulnerable to COVID-19.

Schools' future involvement in multi-agency working

The initial impetus for the research carried out for this book was to investigate the impact of academisation on schools' involvement in multi-agency working in relation to safeguarding and child protection. The promotion of the greater autonomy of schools under the policy potentially created a tension with safeguarding and child protection policies where local authorities are charged with promoting more integrated multi-agency working in line with the principles of *Working Together* (DfE, 2018a). Significantly, we found no evidence in the 58 schools we visited to suggest that academies and local authority-maintained schools approached their safeguarding responsibilities differently. The present government remains committed to academisation and the goal for all state-funded schools to join MATs (Williamson, 2021). Furthermore, the rhetoric used to frame this policy and education reforms more generally has continued to emphasise the need to improve classroom teaching and pupil attainment. This is particularly evident in statements that emphasise the need for children to 'catch up' with their learning following extended time out of the classroom during the pandemic. In June 2021 the DfE announced that £1.4 billion, spread over three years, would be invested in tutoring and teacher training (Stewart and Clews, 2021).

On the other hand, the pandemic has placed the spotlight on the broader role that schools play to promote the safety and well-being of children and the importance of multi-agency working in this regard. Many families have faced significant difficulties during the pandemic, and some children and young people will not have received the support and protection previously available to them. In November 2021 a father and his partner were sentenced for the manslaughter and murder respectively of six-year-old Arthur Labinjo-Hughes in June 2020. The government has launched a national review and a Joint Targeted Area Inspection 'to determine what improvements are needed by the agencies that came into contact with him in the months before he died' (DfE, 2021d). In any calculation his experience of family violence meant he was a vulnerable child. The school noted and reported a steady deterioration in Arthur's mental state, but until mid March 2020 he was in school. Children's social care did visit the home in response to anxiety expressed by his grandmother that he had bruises on his back but they were reportedly not concerned. As in so many instances reported to us the school was asked to provide support to the family. The school did conduct welfare checks on Arthur by telephone although the calls were not always answered. When they were told he was fine they seem to have been reassured. When the school reopened after lockdown Arthur did not attend. His father explained the absence by saying the child had sleeping and eating problems. Just over a week later he was killed. A statement from the Association of Child Protection Professionals said:

> 'Arthur's situation appears to have been exacerbated by the pandemic, and the impact that lock-down restrictions had on vulnerable children and social care services. It happened at a time when services were having to rapidly change the way they worked. Taking children like Arthur out of the school routine risked making them invisible to professionals and services and made other possible routes for intervention very difficult to access.' (Simpson, 2021)

We can be confident that for many of the schools we visited, addressing the impact of the pandemic on safeguarding and mental health will be just as important as catching up with lost learning. However, this is likely to place additional pressure on already stretched school resources. Significantly, the government's Education Recovery Commissioner Sir Kevan Collins resigned immediately after the announcement on funding for tutoring and teacher training in June 2021. Collins had called for a much broader £15 billion package of measures incorporating sport, music and other activities to support re-engagement in education (Stewart and Clews, 2021).

Beyond the question of funding, the extent to which schools are represented at a strategic level under new local multi-agency safeguarding arrangements could also be an important determinant of how safeguarding policies and working practices develop in the coming years. It should be recalled that at the time we visited schools for this research, local areas were in the process of establishing new multi-agency safeguarding arrangements to replace LSCBs as recommended by Sir Alan Wood (Wood, 2016). Staff we spoke with expressed concern about how the views of schools would be represented under the new arrangements centred around the three named safeguarding partners, local authorities, health and the police. Informants in Driscoll et al's (2021) study were also concerned about what they perceived as the marginalisation of schools. Following an initial review of the new arrangements, Wood (2021) acknowledged that the engagement of schools had emerged as a specific issue to be addressed. He argued that examples of successful engagement had been found but conceded that '[m]ore can and should be done to ensure head teachers and designated leads in schools can work effectively with the local arrangements and where possible find a consensual view from the broad range of schools in any area' (Wood, 2021, p 8). However, the study reported in this book, and one previously conducted with LSCBs (Baginsky and Holmes, 2015), the precursor to multi-agency partnership arrangements, identified few problems with schools working with local arrangements; rather the challenges were in establishing manageable approaches to representation.

The findings presented in this book have also shown how the range of specific safeguarding problems to which schools must respond has grown over recent years. Moreover, when specific concerns have been identified and reported on in the media Ministers have invariably looked to schools to play a part in addressing these concerns. Thus, in recent years many schools have become increasingly engaged in work to support the mental health of young people and the related issue of online safety and social media use. In the coming years schools will need to address specific concerns relating to peer-on-peer sexual abuse. Ofsted has conducted a review of how schools deal with cases of peer-on-peer sexual abuse following widespread media reporting of the problem in early 2021 (Ofsted, 2021). Among its findings was that sexual harassment is a routine occurrence in schools and that girls particularly face a culture that leads to a failure to disclose. According to the report this, in turn, means that schools underestimate the extent of sexual harassment. When we reflected on our discussions in schools, we found we concurred with these findings. We had visited schools during 2018 and 2019 and although peer-on-peer abuse was highlighted as a concern by some staff in secondary schools it was generally discussed in the wider context of online safety.

At the time of writing the House of Commons Education Committee was also preparing a report on its inquiry into home education. This is an area of policy that the Child Safeguarding Review Panel (2021) has identified as a priority for it to investigate. Local authorities spoken to and surveyed during the research for this book highlighted the limited powers they had to ensure the safeguarding of children educated at home. Participants in Driscoll et al's (2021) study expressed concern regarding increases in the number of parents choosing to educate children at home following the enforced periods of home learning during the pandemic.

More generally, participants in Baginsky and Manthorpe's (2020b) study raised the problem of 'initiative fatigue'. However, it is highly likely that schools seeking to balance their teaching and wider pastoral responsibilities in the years to come will continue to do so in the context of a steady stream of new policy reviews and reform initiatives supported by time-limited ring-fenced funding at best. The outcome of the delayed DfE review of Special Educational Needs and Disabilities (SEND) will arguably have the most direct bearing on funding and practice in schools. In addition, other major reviews, such as the ongoing Independent Review of Children's Social Care, could also have important implications for schools and multi-agency safeguarding work more widely.

APPENDIX 1

Congruence analysis of the national surveys of education, children's social care and Local Safeguarding Children Boards

As explained in Chapter 1, we analysed the survey findings to help to identify the five local authority areas where the case studies involving schools would be carried out. We wanted to identify groups of local authorities which, based on the survey data, displayed varying degrees of 'congruence' in the responses provided across education, children's social care and LSCBs. In 39 local authority areas all three agencies responded to our surveys. However, in four of these areas two of the surveys had been completed by the same person and in a further three areas there were too many 'don't know' responses. This left 32 authorities that had provided a full set of responses from the three agencies.

Question scoring

A total of 17 questions were asked in all three of the surveys, which could be broadly grouped under the following headings:

- Safeguarding
- Child sexual exploitation
- Thresholds
- Satisfaction with local authority support
- Views on national safeguarding guidance and inspection criteria

The questions used in the cluster analysis are provided in Table A1.1.

Table A1.1: Questions used in cluster analysis

Safeguarding

Are raising awareness and understanding of the children's services threshold document included in training for schools Designated Safeguarding Leads (DSLs)?

Is your authority a pilot area for Operation Encompass?

To which service are schools expected to make a child protection referral?

Child sexual exploitation

Does the local authority employ a dedicated team/individual to respond to CSE concerns?

Has the local authority devised a CSE risk assessment tool for use by school-based staff?

In your view, how satisfied are local schools about the way in which concerns raised about possible CSE are responded to by the local authority?

How are schools expected to raise concerns regarding possible CSE?

National frameworks

To what extent do you consider that Keeping Children Safe in Education (DfE, 2016) is fit for purpose?

To what extent do you think the introduction of Ofsted's (2015) Common Inspection Framework has had an impact on safeguarding practice in schools?

To what extent do you think the joint Care Quality Commission/Ofsted (2016) Local Area Special Educational Needs and/or Disabilities (SEND) Inspection Framework has had an impact on safeguarding practice in schools?

Thresholds

Please rate awareness and understanding of thresholds operating in children's services amongst local schools.

Comparing 2017 with 2012, how would you assess thresholds for section 47 referrals?

Comparing 2017 with 2012, how would you assess thresholds for section 17 referrals?

Satisfaction with local authority

In your view, how satisfied are local schools about the way in which section 47 referrals are responded to by the local authority?

In your view, how satisfied are local schools about the way in which section 17 referrals are responded to by the local authority?

In your view, how satisfied are local schools about the way in which concerns raised about online safety/social media are responded to by the local authority?

How satisfied do you think local schools are about the way in which the local authority has responded to concerns raised about radicalisation?

For questions where the response was nominal (that is, there is no intrinsic ordering to the categories), a scoring system of 0 for no matches, 1 for one match and 3 for all matches was used. This scoring system was logical as it provided a point for each relationship in which there was a match, as demonstrated in Table A1.2.

Where a respondent had marked a question as Don't know the default score for that match was 0.

For questions where the response was ordinal (that is, where there is a clear ordering of the categories) we calculated a score for each possible match based on how close the responses were to each other on the scale. For example, one of the questions used the following scale:

- Not at all
- To a limited extent
- Adequate
- Good
- Excellent
- Don't know

If this was treated in the same manner as the nominal responses then a response of Good compared to one of Excellent would score the same in terms of congruence as a response of Not at all compared to Excellent, despite the former being definably more congruent than the latter. We therefore scaled all nominal questions so that each relationship scored on a scale of 0 (where responses were at both extremes – 1 and 5 in the earlier example) to 1 (where both responded with the same rating). Again, where a respondent had marked a question as Don't know the default score for that match was 0.

This meant that now a response of Good compared to Excellent would score 0.75 while a score of Not at all to Excellent would score 0. This method also ensured that the maximum score for any one question would be 3 so all questions were weighted evenly in the scoring.

Table A1.2: Nominal question scoring in cluster analysis

Survey 1	Survey 2	All match	Education and social care match	Education and LSCB	Social care and LSCB match	No matches
Education	Social Care	1	1	0	0	0
Education	LSCB	1	0	1	0	0
Social Care	LSCB	1	0	0	1	0

Education/social care weighting

Given the direct relationship between schools and children's social care over referrals and other aspects of family-based multi-agency work, it was decided that congruence between education and social care should be given greater weight within the model than congruence with LSCBs. Once the scores for each responder had been calculated, any points gained from congruence between social care and education were given a weight of 2 (compared to education & LSCB and social care & LSCB, which both had a weight of 1).

Don't know scores

Alongside the score for congruence we also calculated a score for Don't knows – one point was awarded each time a respondent from any of the three surveys did not answer a question or answered Don't know. This allowed us to see when a low congruence score had been impacted by incomplete or uncertain responses. In the final modelling we excluded all areas with a 'don't know' score of more than 10, which resulted in the exclusion of nine areas (seven of which were clustered in the very low congruence group due to the impact of low data quality on their matching scores).

Clustering approaches

We undertook hierarchical cluster modelling in SPSS, with the number of clusters specified as five (which is what was required for the case study selection). This was done both with overall score and with individual congruence variable scores to test whether this impacted the model. The model based on the total score provided more defined and evenly distributed clusters so this was chosen as the appropriate input. We used Squared Euclidian Distance as the distance measure, as it increases the importance of large distances, while weakening the importance of small distances.

We tested the model with various cluster methods (including between-groups linkage, nearest neighbour, centroid, median and Ward's method). Using different clustering methods (particularly nearest neighbour) helped to identify one of the respondent areas as an outlier that needed to be removed from the final model. Ward's minimum variance method (Kaufman and Rousseeuw, 1990) provided the best clustering so was used as the cluster method for the final model, which included a total of 23 areas after areas with high 'don't know' scores had been removed (Table A1.3).

As explained in Chapter 1, one area from each of the five congruence groups was then selected for the case studies, with the overall aim to arrive at a set of case study areas representing different regions, local authority type and size, and socio-economic context.

Table A1.3: Final cluster scores

Congruence group	Local authority	Cluster analysis score
Very low	LA 1	26.8
	LA 2	31.9
	LA 3	32.3
Low	LA 4	35.1
	LA 5	35.3
	LA 6	36.0
	LA 7	36.4
	LA 8	36.9
Medium	LA 9	39.8
	LA 10	40.3
	LA 11	40.3
	LA 12	41.6
	LA 13	43.3
High	LA 14	44.7
	LA 15	44.7
	LA 16	44.8
	LA 17	45.3
	LA 18	46.5
	LA 19	47.6
Very high	LA 20	49.3
	LA 21	50.0
	LA 22	50.7
	LA 23	55.0

APPENDIX 2

The case study schools

Table A2.1 shows the 58 case study schools included four infant/junior schools, 29 primary schools (of which 11 were academies), 19 secondary schools (of which 13 were academies) and five special schools.

Socio-economic context of schools

The socio-economic context of school communities was also considered during the recruitment process. Two indicators of economic disadvantage were used as set out in Table A2.2 and Table A2.3.

Table A2.1: Overview of schools visited by type

	Maintained schools*						Academy schools**					
	Infant	Junior	Primary	Secondary	All through	Special	Infant	Junior	Primary	Secondary	All through	Special
London Borough			4	1	1		1	1		2		
Rural Unitary			4	2	1				1	2		
Middle County	1		1	1					4	2		1
Northern City	1		5	1	1					2		
NorthernUnitary			4	1	1				1	2	1	
MAT									5	3		
Total	2		18	6	4		1	1	11	13	1	1

Notes: *Includes community schools, voluntary aided schools and foundation schools; ** includes free schools, sponsor-led and converter Academies

Table A2.2: Schools by percentage of pupils claiming free school meals

	40% +	30–39%	20–29%	10–19%	0–9%
London Borough		1	1	8	
Rural Unitary			1	1	8
Middle County		2		2	6
Northern City	5	2	1	1	1
Northern Unitary	2	1	2	4	1
MAT	3		2	3	
Total	10	6	7	19	16

Source: Department for Education, 2019

Table A2.3: Schools by Index of Deprivation Affecting Children Index (IDACI)

	IDACI decile based on school postcode (1 = top 10%)									
	1	2	3	4	5	6	7	8	9	10
London Borough	1	5	2	1	1					
Rural Unitary			1				4	1	2	2
Middle County				2	1	1	3		2	1
Northern City	3	4	1		1			1		
Northern Unitary	1	3		1	2		2			1
MAT	5	1			1		1			
Total	10	13	4	4	6	1	10	2	4	4

Source: Department for Communities and Local Government, 2015

APPENDIX 3

Qualitative Comparative Analysis of the case study interview data

As explained in Chapter 1, the interview data were analysed using thematic analysis (Braun and Clark, 2006). However, we also used Qualitative Comparative Analysis (QCA) (see Ragin, 1987; 2000) to explore possible causal relationships between the themes identified through the thematic analysis.

QCA is a method of evaluating qualitative data that explores the causal relationship between conditions and outcomes using Boolean algebra to implement principles of comparison and is based on set theory. In QCA, every case (in this instance a school) is conceived as a combination of conditions and one particular outcome. QCA enables the identification of conditions (or combinations of conditions) that are necessary and/or sufficient for an outcome to occur.

The outcome of focus for the QCA was the support provided to schools by external agencies (social care, education and LSCB in particular). Specifically, the QCA examined whether:

1. the identified congruence between social care, education and LSCB impacted the support provided to schools by those agencies;
2. there were other factors which affected the support schools received from external agencies;
3. better support from external agencies had an impact on schools' experience of referrals or the degree to which thresholds are understood in schools.

To do this, the interview data were used to create outcome sets. Some sets were defined as crisp sets (which means membership values are either 0 or 1: a school is either a full member of the set or is not) while others were fuzzy sets (where there were five degrees of membership). The interview data were used to score four fuzzy outcome sets (experience of inter-agency working, interaction with LSCB, level of support from the local authority, experience of referrals) and two crisps sets (clarity of thresholds and knowledge of threshold document). The set definitions for the four fuzzy outcome sets are provided in the Table A3.1.

We then defined several conditions that might impact these outcomes (including area congruence, academy status, deprivation, social worker turnover, school phase and Ofsted rating).

Table A3.1: QCA set definitions

Outcome/condition	Description	Anchor points
Experience of inter-agency working	Is there evidence that the DSL feels school is treated as an equal partner, is able to access 'most' agencies and says communication works well?	0: DSL mentioned engaging in multi-agency working and reported mainly negative experiences. 0.5: DSL mentioned engaging in multi-agency working but was neutral/mixed in their experiences. 1: DSL mentioned engaging in multi-agency work with a number of agencies and reported overall positive experiences.
Interaction with LSCB	Is the DSL aware of the LSCB role in training and audits, and are they engaged in LSCB activities and resources?	0: DSL was not aware of LSCB role beyond vague mention of training or audits. 0.5: DSL was engaged with LSCB but not aware of all functions. 1: DSL mentioned LSCB involvement in training, audits and other engagement.
Level of support from local authority	Does the DSL think the local authority provides accessible and useful advice and good support for DSLs (including network meetings, supervision)?	0: DSL reported that the support received from the local authority was inadequate or non-existent. 0.5: DSL reported some support from local authority but quality was inconsistent. 1: DSL reported receiving good and consistent support from the local authority.
Experience of referrals	Are referrals dealt with in a responsive/timely manner, with clear school involvement, and good communication/feedback?	0: DSL was negative about all aspects of the referral process. 0.5: DSL had mixed experience of referrals, with some positive and some negative comments. 1: DSL was positive about referrals in terms of responsiveness/timeliness, communication, actions and feeling engaged/involved in the process.

There are two main measures for the parameters of fit in QCA: consistency and coverage. Consistency represents the extent to which a causal combination leads to an outcome and ranges from 0 to 1. With crisp set outcomes, it is calculated as the proportion of cases with a given causal combination that are also in the outcome set. For fuzzy outcome sets the concept is the same, although the calculation is more complex (Legewie, 2013). Coverage represents the proportion of cases with the outcome that are represented by a particular causal condition. We used fsQCA software for analysis (Ragin et al, 2006).

As recommended in Schneider and Wagemann (2010), we first tested each of the outcomes for necessary conditions. None of the outcomes had any necessary conditions.

Truth table analysis was undertaken for each outcome, first with only the congruence and academy sets, then with congruence and other outcomes, and lastly with any combinations of conditions and outcomes which had resulted in a solution with consistency score of more than 0.8. This same analysis was undertaken on the negation of each outcome.

The analysis used the following simplifying rules:

- each causal combination had to have more than one member (which meant excluding any recipes with 1 or 0 occurrences);
- any causal combination with consistency of 0.75 or more was taken to be initially consistent with the outcome, unless there were multiple consistency scores of 0.85 or more, in which case anything under 0.85 was treated as inconsistent;
- the overall solution consistency should be equal to or above 0.8, with coverage over 0.5 to be deemed to have sufficient explanatory power for the solution to be worth reporting.

Where QCA found a notable relationship following these rules, it is reported in the text of the book. Only two outcomes were found to have causal relationships by the QCA:

- level of support from local authority and interaction with LSCB; and
- experience of referrals and experience of inter-agency working.

The consistency and coverage scores for these relationships are provided in the main body of the book along with XY plots of the fuzzy sets. Single points in the plot show individual cases. Cases sharing the same values are combined to a single, larger point.

APPENDIX 4

Working environment in schools

As detailed in Chapter 1 we used the Organisational Structural Context (OSC) instrument to enable us to produce a profile of the working environment within each of the schools.

Of the 58 schools involved in the case studies, staff from 56 schools completed the OSC instrument. However, as the analysis required the completion of at least three instruments in each school, data were analysed for only 48 schools. The OSC is used to provide profiles of the Culture (made up of 'proficiency', 'rigidity' and 'resistance') and Climate (made up of 'engagement', 'functionality' and 'stress') of an organisation, in this case a school.

The culture items measure teachers' self-reported expectations about how they should behave. So, for example, 'high rigidity' would suggest staff expected less discretion and flexibility in their work; 'high resistance' would indicate an expectation that new ideas were suppressed, resulting in few opportunities for change; and 'low proficiency' suggested staff did not think it was important for their management that they have up-to-date knowledge or place the well-being of pupils first. This means that 'low rigidity', 'low resistance' and 'high proficiency' would be the reverse.

The climate items measure teachers' experience of the impact of their working environment on their own well-being. 'Low engagement' indicated that staff are less likely to feel they have achieved meaningful results with their pupils and less likely to report that their efforts were worthwhile; 'low functionality' indicated they do not feel they are provided the right tools to do their job properly; and 'high stress' indicated the staff are emotionally exhausted, conflicted in their role and overloaded with work. Again, 'high engagement', 'high functionality' and 'low stress' would demonstrate the reverse.

The rWG values (which are an index of agreement among respondents within a group, in this case a school), for all but one area averaged above 0.9. The rWG is considered acceptable above a value of 0.7 (James et al, 1993), which shows there was a high degree of agreement between participants within each school on each OSC dimension. Each scale also had a coefficient alpha above 0.7, which shows that responses to items within scales were reliable even though they were slightly reworded from the original version of the OSC in order to properly apply to a school and English setting. All school OSC raw scores were converted to T-Scores based on a sample of 100 US mental health agencies (as more comparable OSC data were

Table A4.1: Mean OSC T-Scores by school phases

Congruence	Climate			Culture			No. of schools
	Proficiency (high = good)	Rigidity (low = good)	Resistance (low = good)	Engagement (high = good)	Functionality (high = good)	Stress (low = good)	
Primary	51	50	47	52	52	50	28
Secondary	47	52	56	44	44	53	15
All-through	38	45	47	52	53	41	1
Special	58	46	48	62	57	39	4

not available). A T-Score of 50 represents the average, while a T-Score of $+/-10$ from 50 would be one standard deviation above or below the average. First, to test whether the congruency of agencies (see Appendix 1) within an area had any impact on the organisational profile of the school, we compared the average T-Score for each of the six elements of the OSC across all schools within each congruency area. No significant differences were found between schools based on the degree of congruency in the local area.

Second, the distinction between secondary and primary schools was also examined with significance tested using independent samples T-tests. This confirmed that secondary schools had significantly higher resistance ($p=.009$), and significantly lower engagement ($p = .008$) and functionality ($p = .018$) compared with primary schools, as shown in Table A4.1, indicating a more negative culture and climate in the secondary schools.

Third, we then compared the interview data from the six schools with the most positive OSC profiles with the six with the most negative OSC profiles. Four of the six schools in the positive group were primaries and the other two were special schools. In the more negative category four were secondaries and two were primaries. The key findings were:

• schools in the negative category were more likely to be in areas of high economic deprivation and, in these schools, staff spoke about high levels of need in their communities;
• in schools in the positive category (made up of four primary and two special schools) safeguarding teams were smaller and staff indicated a clear understanding of local thresholds for children's social care;
• in general, schools in the positive category felt better supported by their local authorities and more able to access early help for children and families.

Timeline of schools and children's welfare since 1870

The timeline on the following pages shows how children's rights and state involvement in childcare have evolved in England.

Figure A5.1: Schools and children's welfare since 1870

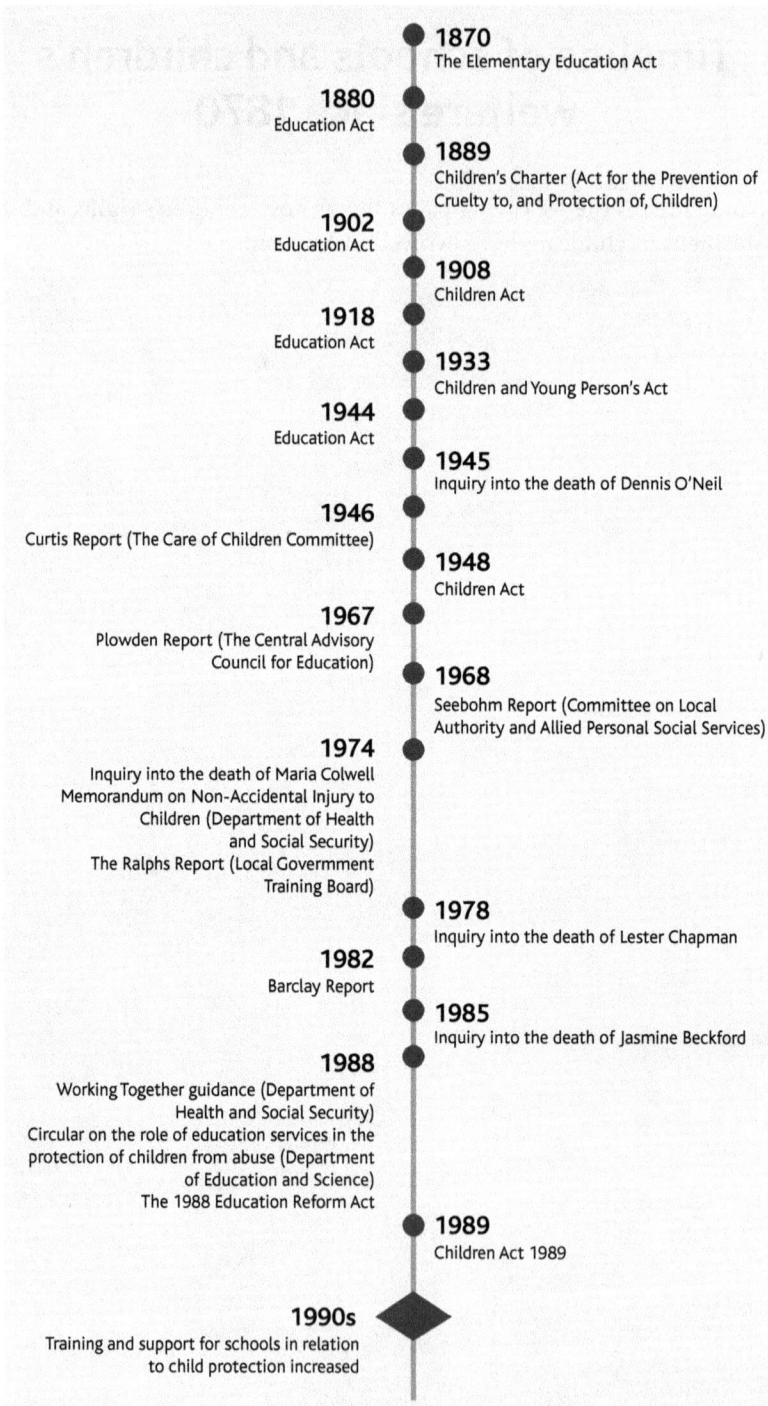

1870
The Elementary Education Act

1880
Education Act

1889
Children's Charter (Act for the Prevention of Cruelty to, and Protection of, Children)

1902
Education Act

1908
Children Act

1918
Education Act

1933
Children and Young Person's Act

1944
Education Act

1945
Inquiry into the death of Dennis O'Neil

1946
Curtis Report (The Care of Children Committee)

1948
Children Act

1967
Plowden Report (The Central Advisory Council for Education)

1968
Seebohm Report (Committee on Local Authority and Allied Personal Social Services)

1974
Inquiry into the death of Maria Colwell
Memorandum on Non-Accidental Injury to Children (Department of Health and Social Security)
The Ralphs Report (Local Govermment Training Board)

1978
Inquiry into the death of Lester Chapman

1982
Barclay Report

1985
Inquiry into the death of Jasmine Beckford

1988
Working Together guidance (Department of Health and Social Security)
Circular on the role of education services in the protection of children from abuse (Department of Education and Science)
The 1988 Education Reform Act

1989
Children Act 1989

1990s
Training and support for schools in relation to child protection increased

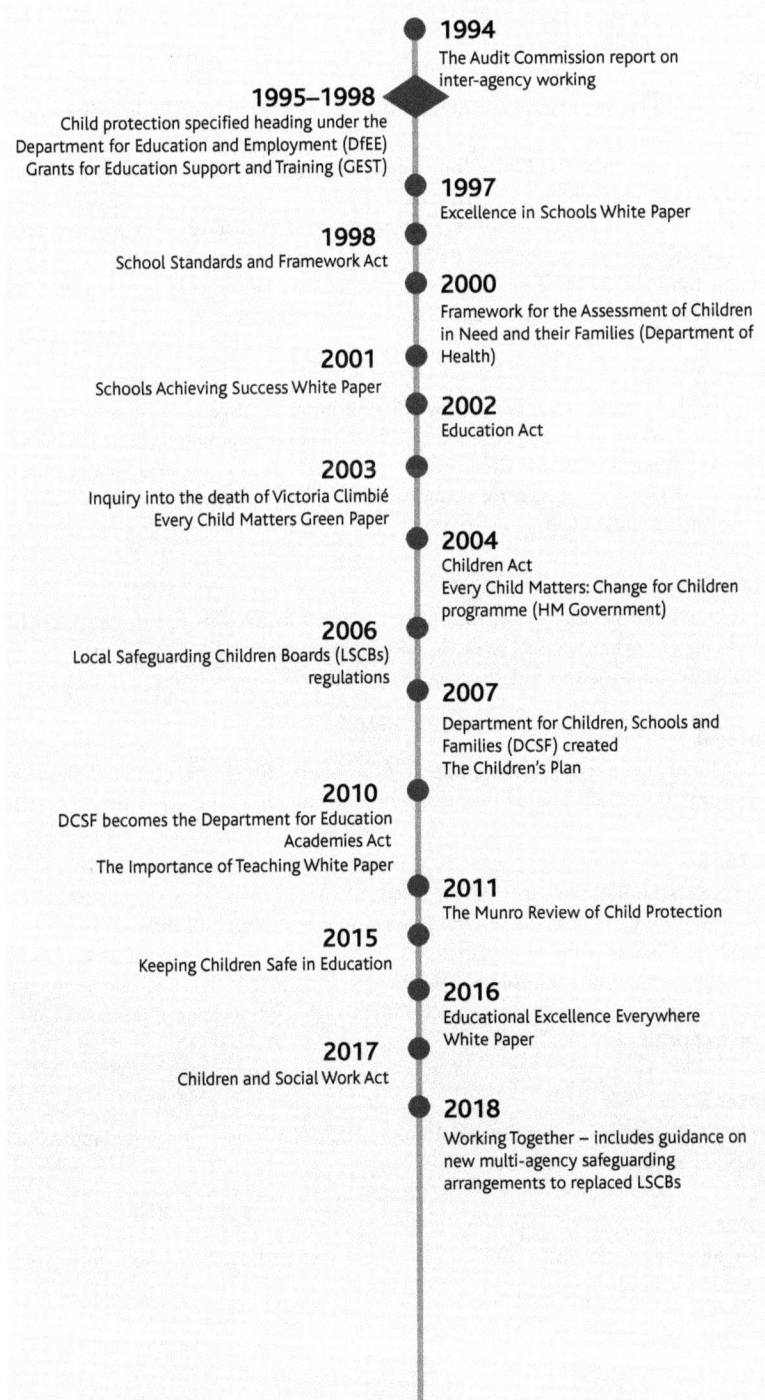

1994
The Audit Commission report on inter-agency working

1995–1998
Child protection specified heading under the Department for Education and Employment (DfEE) Grants for Education Support and Training (GEST)

1997
Excellence in Schools White Paper

1998
School Standards and Framework Act

2000
Framework for the Assessment of Children in Need and their Families (Department of Health)

2001
Schools Achieving Success White Paper

2002
Education Act

2003
Inquiry into the death of Victoria Climbié
Every Child Matters Green Paper

2004
Children Act
Every Child Matters: Change for Children programme (HM Government)

2006
Local Safeguarding Children Boards (LSCBs) regulations

2007
Department for Children, Schools and Families (DCSF) created
The Children's Plan

2010
DCSF becomes the Department for Education
Academies Act
The Importance of Teaching White Paper

2011
The Munro Review of Child Protection

2015
Keeping Children Safe in Education

2016
Educational Excellence Everywhere White Paper

2017
Children and Social Work Act

2018
Working Together – includes guidance on new multi-agency safeguarding arrangements to replaced LSCBs

Notes

Chapter 1

[1] The 2021 data reflect the impact of COVID-19 and, as such, are not directly comparable with previous years.

[2] The inspection body, the Office for Standards in Education, whose remit was extended in 2007 to include children's social care.

[3] A 'multi-academy trust' (MAT) is a group of schools that are in a partnership with each other.

[4] At the time children's services were merged across Westminster and Kensington and Chelsea, and across Richmond and Kingston upon Thames.

Chapter 2

[1] This has now changed. Under Ofsted's 2019 Education Inspection Framework (EIF) in order for a school to be judged good or better, then safeguarding must be deemed to be effective. While ineffective safeguarding will usually lead to an inadequate judgement the new EIF allows inspectors, under certain circumstances, to issue a Requires Improvement judgement.

Chapter 3

[1] This is an estimate for periods outside of national lockdowns during the COVID-19 pandemic and when schools were closed to most pupils.

[2] This study did not cover independent or private fee-paying schools.

Chapter 4

[1] The Model of Supervision is based upon Wonnacott's (2012) model and is designed to be a practical tool which helps to promote reflective supervision for use with social workers.

Chapter 5

[1] The eight schools within the MAT case study were in six different local authority areas and it was not clear how the referral process operated in each of these areas.

[2] Please see Chapter 3 for an explanation of tiers 1–4 in children's social care.

[3] No other condition improved the QCA solution for positive referrals; although the congruence of an area increased the consistency (to 0.98) it reduced the coverage to less than half of all cases (0.42).

Chapter 6

[1] In 2020–21 one day a week of family support worker time cost schools approximately £6,500 per year.

Chapter 7

[1] This initiative lasted from 1988 to 1998 and involved 1,196 schools, most of them secondary schools.

References

Alfandari, R. (2019) Multi-professional work in child protection decision-making: An Israeli case study. *Children and Youth Services Review*, 98, 51–7.

Allen-Kinross, P. (2019) Tighten rules on parental consultation before academy conversion, DfE told. *Schools Week*, 12 July.

Anning, A., Cottrell, D., Frost, N., Green, J. and Robinson, M. (2006) *Developing Multiprofessional Teamwork for Integrated Children's Services*. Maidenhead: Open University Press.

Association of Directors of Children's Services (2018) *Safeguarding Pressures Phase 6 Research Report*. Manchester: Association of Directors of Children's Services.

Association of Directors of Children's Services (2019) *Elective Home Education Survey 2019*. Manchester: Association of Directors of Children's Services.

Association of Directors of Children's Services (2020) *ADCS Elective Home Education Survey 2020*. Manchester: Association of Directors of Children's Services.

Association of Directors of Children's Services (2021) *ADCS Elective Home Education Survey 2021*. Manchester: Association of Directors of Children's Services.

Association of Directors of Social Services (ADSS) (1978) *Social Work Services for Children in Schools*. London: ADSS.

Atkinson, M., Doherty, P. and Kinder, K. (2005) Multi-agency working. Models, challenges and key factors for success. *Journal of Early Childhood Research*, 3, 1, 7–17.

Audit Commission (1994) *Watching their Figures*. London: HMSO.

Baginsky, M. (2000) *Child Protection and Education*. London: NSPCC.

Baginsky, M. (2003) *Responsibility Without Power*. London: NSPCC.

Baginsky, M. (2005) *Evaluation of NSPCC's School Teams* (unpublished – available from author).

Baginsky, M. (2007) *Schools, Social Services and Safeguarding Children: Past Practice and Future Challenges*. London: NSPCC.

Baginsky, M. (2018) *Integrated Care and Support for Children: Analysis of Practices*. Brussels: European Social Network.

Baginsky, M., Driscoll, J., Manthorpe, J. and Purcell, C. (2019) Perspectives on safeguarding and child protection in English schools: The new educational landscape explored. *Educational Research*, 61, 4, 469–81.

Baginsky, M. and Holmes, D. (2015) *A Review of Current Arrangements for the Operation of Local Safeguarding Children Boards*. London: Local Government Association.

Baginsky, M. and Manthorpe, J. (2020a) The impact of COVID-19 on children's social care in England. *Child Abuse and Neglect*, https://doi.org/10.1016/j.chiabu.2020.104739

Baginsky, M. and Manthorpe, J. (2020b) Keeping children and young people safe during a pandemic: Testing the robustness of multi-agency child protection and safeguarding arrangements for schools. NIHR Policy Research Unit in Health and Social Care Workforce, The Policy Institute, King's College London.

Baginsky, M. and Manthorpe, J. (2021) Multiagency working between children's social care and schools during COVID-19: Case study experiences from English local authorities and international reflections. *Journal of Integrated Care*, https://doi.org/10.1108/JICA-01-2021-0004

Baginsky, M., Teague, C., Emsley, L., Price, C., Sames, K. and Truong, Y. (2011) A *Summative Report on the Qualitative Evaluation on the Eleven Remodelling Pilots*. Leeds: Children's Workforce Development Council.

Ball, S. (2021) *The Education Debate: Fourth Edition*. Bristol: Policy Press.

Barclay, P. (1982) *Social Workers: Their Roles and Tasks*. London: Bedford Square Press.

Barnes, J. and Melhuish, E. with Guera, J. C., Karwowska-Struczyk, M. K. Petrogiannis, K., Wyslowska, O. and Zachrisson, H. D. (2017) *Inter-Agency Coordination of Services for Children and Families – Initial Literature Review*. Brussels: Inclusive Education and Social Support to Tackle Inequalities in Society (ISOTIS).

Beddoe, L. and de Haan, I. (2018) Addressing concerns about child maltreatment in schools: A brief research report on social work involvement in reporting processes. *Aotearoa New Zealand Social Work*, 30, 1, 58–64.

Bell, M. M. and Singh, M. I. (2017) Implementing a collaborative support model for educators reporting child maltreatment. *Children and Schools*, 39, 7–14.

Bennett, D, L., Schlüter, D. K., Melis, G., Bywaters, P., Barr, B., Wickham, S. and Taylor-Robinson, D. C. (2022) Child poverty and children entering care: A natural experiment using longitudinal area-level data in England, 2015–2020. Available at SSRN: https://ssrn.com/abstract=3972210 or http://dx.doi.org/10.2139/ssrn.3972210

Bernstein, B. (1970) Education cannot compensate for society. *New Society*, 15, 387, 344–7.

Body, A. (2020) *Children's Charities in Crisis: Early Intervention and the State*. Bristol: Policy Press.

Brandon, M., Howe, A., Dagley, V., Salter, C. and Warren, C. (2006) What appears to be helping or hindering practitioners in implementing the Common Assessment Framework and lead professional working? *Child Abuse Review*, 15, 6, 396–413.

Braun, D. (1988) *Responding to Child Abuse: Action and Planning for Teachers and Other Professionals*. London: Bedford Square Press.

Braun, V. and Clarke, V. (2006) Using thematic analysis in psychology. *Qualitative Research in Psychology*, 3, 2, 77–101.

Brindle, D. (2009) No one said it would be easy. *The Guardian*, 28 January.

Brown, R. (2018) *Mental Health and Wellbeing Provision in Schools: Review of Published Policies and Information*. London: Department for Education.

Bunting, L., Lazenbatt, A. and Wallace, I. (2010) Information sharing and reporting systems in the UK and Ireland: Professional barriers to reporting child maltreatment concerns. *Child Abuse Review*, 19, 187–202.

Butler, P. (2014) How Alan Wood became the 'go-to fixer' for child protection. *The Guardian*, 9 July.

Butler-Sloss, E. (1988) *Report of the Inquiry into Child Abuse in Cleveland 1987*. London: HMSO.

Bywaters, P., Brady, G., Bunting, L., Daniel, B., Featherstone, B., Jones, C., Morris, K., Scourfield, J., Sparks, T. and Webb, C. (2018) Inequalities in English child protection practice under austerity: A universal challenge? *Child and Family Social Work*, 23, 1, 53–61.

Bywaters, P., Bunting, L., Davidson, G., Hanratty, J., Mason, W., McCartan, C. and Steils, N. (2016) *The Relationship between Poverty, Child Abuse and Neglect: An Evidence Review*. York: Joseph Rowntree Foundation.

Bywaters, P., Scourfield, J., Jones, C., Sparks, T., Elliott, M., Hooper, J., Mccartan, C., Shapira, M., Bunting, L. and Daniel, B. (2020) Child welfare inequalities in the four nations of the UK. *Journal of Social Work*, 2, 193–215.

Cameron, A. and Lart, R. (2003) Factors promoting and obstacles hindering joint working: A systematic review of the research evidence. *Journal of Integrated Care*, 11, 9–17.

Care of Children Committee (Curtis Committee) *Report of the Care of Children Committee*. cmd.6922. London: HMSO.

Carroll, C., Brackenbury, G., Lee, F., Esposito, R. and O'Brien, T. (2020) *Professional Supervision: Guidance for SENCOs and School Leaders*. London: UCL Institute of Education.

Central Advisory Council for Education (1967) *The Plowden Report – Children and their Primary Schools*. London: HMSO.

Central Policy Review Staff (1975) *A Joint Framework for Social Policies*. London: HMSO.

Centre for Cities (2019) *Cities Outlook 2019*. London: Centre for Cities.

Centre for Educational Research and Innovation (1996) *Integrating Services for Children at Risk: Denmark, France, the Netherlands, Sweden, the United Kingdom (England and Wales)*. Paris: Organisation for Economic Co-operation and Development.

Child Safeguarding Review Panel (2021) Annual report 2020: Patterns in practice, key messages and 2021 work programme. The Child Safeguarding Review Panel, https://www.gov.uk/government/organisations/child-safeguarding-practice-review-panel

Children's Commissioner (2019) *Skipping School: Invisible Children.* London: Children's Commissioner for England.

Children's Commissioner (2020) Children's Commissioner for England Creates Local Area Profiles of Child Vulnerability during Covid-19, https://www.childrenscommissioner.gov.uk/2020/04/25/childrens-commissioner-for-england-creates-local-area-profiles-of-child-vulnerability-during-covid-19/#:~:text=The%20Children's%20Commissioner's%20local%20area,those%20in%20overcrowded%20or%20inadequate

Children's Workforce Development Council (CWDC) (2009) *The Team Around the Child (TAC) and the Lead Professional.* Leeds: CWDC.

Cockburn, J. S., King, H. P. F. and McDonnell, K. G. T. (1969) *A History of the County of Middlesex: Volume 1, Physique, Archaeology, Domesday, Ecclesiastical Organization, the Jews, Religious Houses, Education of Working Classes To 1870, Private Education From Sixteenth Century, British History Online,* http://www.british-history.ac.uk/vch/middx/vol1/pp213-240

Cox, F. and Garvin, C. (1970) The relation of social forces to the emergence of community organization practice: 1865–1968 in F. Cox, J. Erlich, J. Rothman and J. Tropman (eds) *Strategies of Community Organization.* Itasca, IL: F. E. Peacock.

Crane, J. (2018) *Child Protection in England 1960–2000.* London: Palgrave Macmillan.

Creighton, S. (1987) Quantitative assessment of child abuse in P. Maher (ed) *Child Abuse: The Educational Perspective.* Oxford: Basil Blackwell.

Crin, R. (2014) *Do Academies Make Use of Their Autonomy?* London: Department for Education.

Crockett, R., Gilchrist, G., Davies, J., Henshall, A., Hoggart, L., Chandler, V., Sims, D. and Webb, J. (2013) *Assessing the Early Impact of Multi Agency Safeguarding Hubs (MASH) in London* . London: London Councils.

Cummins, I. (2018) *Poverty, Inequality and Social Work: The Impact of Neoliberalism and Austerity Politics on Welfare Provision.* Bristol: Policy Press.

Daniel, B., Taylor, J. and Scott, J. (2011) *Recognizing and Helping the Neglected Child: Evidence Based Practice for Assessment and Intervention* London: Jessica Kingsley Publisher.

Davies, C. and Ward, H. (2012) *Safeguarding Children Across Services: Messages from Research.* London: Jessica Kingsley Publisher.

Davies, R. (2015) Home education: Then and now. *Oxford Review of Education,* 41, 4, 534–48.

Dearden, L. (2019) Number of far-right referrals to counter-extremism programme hits record high. *The Independent,* 19 December.

Department for Communities and Local Government (2015) *English Indices of Deprivation 2015*. London: Department for Communities and Local Government.

Department for Education (2010) *The Importance of Teaching: The Schools White Paper 2010*. London: Department for Education.

Department for Education (2016) *Educational Excellence Everywhere*. London: Department for Education.

Department for Education (2018a) *Working Together to Safeguard Children: A Guide to Inter-agency Working to Safeguard and Promote the Welfare of Children*. London: Department for Education.

Department for Education (2018b) Elective home education: Call for evidence, https://consult.education.gov.uk/school-frameworks/home-education-call-for-evidence-and-revised-dfe-a/

Department for Education (2018c) *Experimental Statistics: Children and Family Social Work Workforce in England, Year Ending 30 September 2018*. London: Department for Education.

Department for Education (2019) *Schools, Pupils and their Characteristics: January 2019*. London: Department for Education.

Department for Education (2020a) *Statistics: Children in Need and Child Protection*. London: Department for Education.

Department for Education (2020b) Supporting vulnerable children and young people during the Coronavirus (Covid-19) outbreak – Actions for educational providers and other partners, https://www.gov.uk/government/publications/coronavirus-covid-19-guidance-on-vulnerable-children-and-young-people/coronavirus-covid-19-guidance-on-vulnerable-children-and-young-people

Department for Education (2021a) *Keeping Children Safe in Education*. London: Department for Education.

Department for Education (2021b) *Statistics: Children in Need and Child Protection*. London: Department for Education.

Department for Education (2021c) Attendance in education and early years settings during the coronavirus (COVID-19) outbreak, https://explore-education-statistics.service.gov.uk/find-statistics/attendance-in-education-and-early-years-settings-during-the-coronavirus-covid-19-outbreak/2021-week-19

Department for Education (2021d) Government action following murder of Arthur Labinjo-Hughes, Press release, 5 December, https://www.gov.uk/government/news/government-action-following-murder-of-arthur-labinjo-hughes

Department for Education and Employment (DfEE) (1997) *Excellence in Schools*. London: DfEE.

Department for Education and Employment (DfEE) (1998) *Teaching: High Status, High Standards (Circular 4/98)*. London: DfEE.

Department for Education and Science (DES) (1988) *Working Together for the Protection of Children from Abuse: The Role of Educational Service (Circular 4/88).* London: DES.

Department for Education and Skills (2001) *Schools Achieving Success.* London: Department for Education and Skills.

Department of Health (2002) *Safeguarding Children: A Joint Chief Inspectors' Report on Arrangements to Safeguard Children.* London: Department of Health.

Department of Health and Department for Education (2017) *Transforming Children and Young People's Mental Health Provision.* London: Department of Health and Department for Education.

Department of Health, Department for Education and Employment and Home Office (2000) *Framework for the Assessment of Children in Need and their Families.* London: The Stationery Office.

Department of Health, Home Office and Department for Education and Employment (1999) *Working Together to Safeguard Children: A Guide to Inter-agency Working to Safeguard and Promote the Welfare of Children.* London: The Stationery Office.

Department of Health and Social Security (DHSS) (1974a) *Report of the Committee of Inquiry into the Care and Supervision Provided in Relation to Maria Colwell.* London: HMSO.

Department of Health and Social Security (DHSS) (1974b) *A Memorandum on Non-accidental Injury to Children.* London: Department of Health and Social Security.

Department of Health and Social Security (DHSS) (1987) *The Law on Child Care and Family Services.* London: HMSO.

Department of Health and Social Security (DHSS) (1988) *Working Together: A Guide to Inter-Agency Co-operation for the Protection of Children from Abuse.* London: HMSO.

Dickinson, R. (2019) Let austerity end for the children first. *Management Journal of Local Authority Business*, 28 May.

Dingwell, R., Eekelaar, J. M. and Murray, T. (1984) Childhood as a social problem: A survey of the history of legal regulation. *Journal of Law and Society*, 11, 2, 207–32.

Driscoll, J., Lorek, A., Kinnear, E. and Hutchinson, A. (2020) Multi-agency safeguarding arrangements: Overcoming the challenges of Covid-19 measures. *Journal of Children's Services*, 15, 4, 267–74.

Driscoll, J., Hutchinson, A., Lorek, A. and Kiss, K. (2021) Protecting children at a distance: Summary of findings from Stage 2: A multi-agency investigation of child safeguarding and protection responses consequent upon COVID-19 lock-down/social distancing measures', https://www.kcl.ac.uk/ecs/assets/projects/protecting-children-at-a-distance-executive-summary-of-stage-2-findings-summary-and-conclusions.pdf

Dunne, J. F. and Finalay, F. (2016) G625 Multi-agency safeguarding hub – a new way of working. *Archives of Disease in Childhood*, 101, A369–A370.

The Economist (1943) Spotlight on poverty. *The Economist*, 144, 545–6.

Edwards, A., Barnes, M., Plewis, I. and. Morris, K. (2006) *Working to Prevent the Social Exclusion of Children and Young People: Final Lessons from the National Evaluation of the Children's Fund*. London: DfES Research Report 734.

Edwards, A., Daniels, H., Gallagher, T., Leadbetter, J. and Warmington, P. (2009) *Improving inter-professional collaborations: multi-agency working for children's wellbeing*. London: Routledge.

Edwards, A., Gharbi, R., Berry, A. and Duschinsky, R. (2021) *Supporting and Strengthening Families Through Provision of Early Help*. London: National Children's Bureau.

Farquharson, C., Sibieta, L., Tahir, I. and Waltmann, B. (2021) 2021 *Annual Report on Education Spending in England*. London: Institute of Fiscal Studies.

Ferguson, H. (1992) Cleveland in history: The abused child and child protection 1880–1914 in R. Cooter (ed) *In the Name of the Child: Health and Welfare 1880–1940*. London: Routledge.

Fink, E., Patalay, P. and Sharp, H. (2015) Mental health difficulties in early adolescence: A comparison of two cross-sectional studies in England from 2009–2014. *Journal of Adolescent Health*, 56, 502–7.

Firmin, C. (2017) *Contextual Safeguarding: An Overview of the Operational, Strategic and Conceptual Framework*. Bedford: University of Bedfordshire, https://uobrep.openrepository.com/handle/10547/624844

Friedman, S. R., Reynolds, J., Quan, M. A., Call, S., Crusto, C. A. and Kaufman, J. S. (2007) Measuring changes in interagency collaboration: An examination of the Bridgeport Safe Start Initiative. *Evaluation and Program Planning*, 30, 294–306.

Gallagher-Mackay, K. (2014) The duty to report child abuse and neglect and the paradox of non-compliance: Relational theory and 'compliance' in the human services. *Journal of Law and Policy*, 36, 3, 256–89.

Gamarnikow, E. and Green, A. G. (1999) The third way and social capital: Education action zones and a new agenda for education, parents and community? *International Studies in Sociology of Education*, 9, 1, 3–22.

Giddens, A. (1998) *The Third Way*. Cambridge: Polity.

Gilbert, R., Kemp, A., Thoburn, J., Sidebotham, P., Radford, L., Glaser, D. and MacMillan, H. L. (2009) Recognising and responding to child maltreatment. *The Lancet*, 373(9658), 167–80.

Glisson, C. and Green, P. D. (2011) Organizational climate, services and outcomes in child welfare systems. *Child Abuse and Neglect*, 35, 582–91.

Gove, M. (2012) The failure of child protection and the need for a fresh start, https://www.gov.uk/government/speeches/the-failure-of-child-protection-and-the-need-for-a-fresh-start

Grover, C. (2020) Understanding material assistance in the Children and Young Persons Act 1963: Idealism and classical liberalism in England and Wales. *Qualitative Social Work*, 19, 5–6, 1238–57.

Halford, P. (1994) *The Education Welfare Service / Education Social Work Service in England and Wales: A Critique of its Organisation and Role.* Unpublished MPhil thesis. Southampton: University of Southampton.

Hall, J. (1979) *Report of an independent inquiry commissioned by the County Councils and Area Health Authorities of Berkshire and Hampshire into the death of Lester Chapman.* Reading: Royal County of Berkshire.

Hallett, C. and Birchall, E. (1992) *Coordination and Child Protection: A Review of the Literature.* Edinburgh: HMSO.

Hallett, C. and Stevenson, O. (1980) *Child Abuse: Aspects of Interprofessional Co-operation.* London: George Allen and Unwin.

Halpern, R. (1991) Supportive services for families in poverty: Dilemmas of reform. *Social Services Review*, 65, 3, 343–64.

Hansard (1988) House of Lords Debate, 6 December, vol 502 cc487–540.

Hansard (2016) Schools that Work for Everyone Debate, 12 September, vol 614 cc601–633.

Hastings, A., Bailey, N., Bramley, G. and Gannon, M. (2017) Austerity urbanism in England: The 'regressive redistribution' of local government services and the impact on the poor and marginalised. *Environment and Planning A: Economy and Space*, 49, 9, 2007–24.

HM Government (2003) *Every Child Matters (Green Paper).* London: The Stationery Office.

HM Government (2004) *Every Child Matters: Next Steps.* London: The Stationery Office.

HM Government (2006) *Working Together to Safeguard Children: A Guide to Inter-agency Working to Safeguard and Promote the Welfare of Children.* London: The Stationery Office.

HM Government (2010) *The Coalition: Our Programme for Government.* London: Cabinet Office.

Home Office (1945) *Report by Sir William Monckton on the Circumstances which Led to the Boarding Out of Dennis and Terence O'Neill at Bank Farm, Minsterly and the Steps Taken to Supervise Their Welfare* (Cmd 6636). London: Home Office.

Home Office (2011) *Prevent Strategy.* London: Home Office.

Home Office (2014) *Multi Agency Working and Information Sharing Project: Final Report.* London: Home Office.

Home Office, Department of Health, Department of Education and Science and Welsh Office (1991) *Working Together Under the Children Act 1989: A Guide to Arrangements for Inter-Agency Co-operation for the Protection of Children from Abuse.* London: HMSO.

Hood, R., Goldacre, A., Gorin, S. and Bywaters, P. (2020) Screen, ration and churn: Demand management and the crisis in children's social care. *The British Journal of Social Work*, 50, 868–89.

Horn, P. (2010) *The Victorian and Edwardian Schoolchild*. Stroud: Amberley Publishing.

Horwath, J. and Morrison, T. (2007) Collaboration, integration and change in children's services: Critical issues and key ingredients. *Child Abuse and Neglect*, 31, 1, 55–69.

Horwath, J. and Morrison, T. (2011) Effective inter-agency collaboration to safeguard children: Rising to the challenge through collective development. *Children and Youth Services Review*, 33, 2, 368–375.

House of Commons Children's Schools and Families Select Committee (2009) *Training of Children and Families Social Workers*. London: House of Commons.

House of Commons Committee of Public Accounts (2015) *School Oversight and Intervention. Thirty-second Report of Session 2014–15*. London: House of Commons.

House of Commons: Housing, Communities and Local Government Committee (2019) *Funding of Local Authorities' Children's Services*. London: House of Commons.

House of Lords Public Services Committee (2021) *The Role of Public Services in Addressing Child Vulnerability*. London: UK Parliament.

Independent Jersey Care Inquiry (2014) *Independent Jersey Care Inquiry Report*. Jersey: Independent Jersey Care Inquiry.

Intriligator, B. A. (1990) Designing effective inter-organisational networks. Paper presented at the annual meeting of the University Council for Educational Administration, Minneapolis.

Jay, A. (2014) *Independent Inquiry into Child Sexual Exploitation in Rotherham (1997–2013)*, https://www.rotherham.gov.uk/downloads/download/31/independent-inquiry-into-child-sexual-exploitation-in-rotherham-1997---2013

James, L. R., Demaree, R. G. and Wolf, G. (1993) rwg: An assessment of within-group interrater agreement. *Journal of Applied Psychology*, 78(2), 306–309. https://doi.org/10.1037/0021-9010.78.2.306

Jennings, H. (1947) Voluntary social services in urban areas in H. Mess (ed) *Voluntary Social Services since 1918*. London: Kegan Paul.

Jones. C. and Leverett, S. (2008) 'Policy into practice: Assessment, evaluation and multi-agency working with children' in P. Foley and A. Rixon (eds) *Changing Children's Services: Working and Learning Together*. Bristol: Policy Press.

Jones, D. N. and Blyth, M. (2016) Does child protection need a rethink? *The Guardian*, 13 January.

Joseph Rowntree Foundation (2021) *UK Poverty 2020–21*. York: Joseph Rowntree Foundation.

Kagan, S. L. (1993) *Integrating Services for Children and Families: Understanding the Past to Shape the Future*. New Haven, CT: Yale University Press.

Kahn, A. J. and Kamerman, S. B. (1992) *Integrating Services Integration: An Overview of Initiatives, Issues and Possibilities*. New York: Columbia University.

Kaufman, L. and Rousseeuw, P. J. (1990) *Finding Groups in Data: An Introduction to Cluster Analysis*. Chichester: John Wiley.

Krugman, P. (2015) The case for cuts was a lie. Why does Britain still believe it? *The Guardian*, 29 April, www.theguardian.com/business/ng-interactive/2015/apr/29/the-austerity-delusion

Labour Party (1997) *New Labour. Because Britain Deserves Better. Election Manifesto*. London: Labour Party.

Laming, W. H. (2003) *The Victoria Climbié Inquiry: Report of an Inquiry by Lord Laming* (Cm. 5730). London: The Stationery Office.

Lancet (1943) An urban close-up. *Lancet*, i, 631.

Leadbetter, J. (2008) Learning in and for interagency working: Making links between practice development and structured reflection. *Learning in Health and Social Care*, 7, 4, 198–208.

Leathard, A. (1994) *Going Inter-professional for Health and Welfare*. London: Routledge.

Legewie, N. (2013) An introduction to applied data analysis with qualitative comparative analysis (QCA). *Forum: Qualitative Social Research*, 14, 3, https://www.qualitative-research.net/index.php/fqs/article/view/1961

Leiba, T. and Weinstein, J. (2003) Who are the participants in the collaborative process and what makes collaboration succeed or fail? In J. Weinstein, C. Whittington and T. Leiba (eds) *Collaboration in Social Work Practice*. London: Jessica Kingsley.

Lessof, C., Ross, A., Brind, R., Bell, E. and Newton, S. (2016) *Longitudinal Study of Young People in England Cohort 2: Health and Wellbeing at Wave 2*. London: Department of Education.

LGA (2019) *Children's Social Care Budgets: A Survey of Lead Members for Children's Services*, February 2019: Local Government Association (LGA) Research and Information.

Local Government Training Board (1974) *Ralphs Report: The Role and Training of Education Welfare Officers*. London: HMSO.

London Borough of Brent (1985) *A Child in Trust: The Report of the Panel of Inquiry into the Circumstances Surrounding the Death of Jasmine Beckford*. London: London Borough of Brent.

Lucas, S. and Archard, P. J. (2021) Early help and children's services: Exploring provision and practice across English local authorities. *Journal of Children's Services*, 16, 1, 74–86.

Maher, P. (ed) (1987) *Child Abuse: The Educational Perspective*. Oxford: Basil Blackwell.

McDonald, J., Murphy, A. and Payne, W. (2001) Ballarat Health Consortium: A case study of influential factors in the development and maintenance of a health partnership. *Australian Journal of Primary Health*, 7, 2, 75–82.

McTavish, J. R., Kimber, M., Devries, K., Colombini, M., MacGregor, J. C. D. and Wathen, C. (2017) Mandated reporters' experiences with reporting child maltreatment: A meta-synthesis of qualitative studies. *BMJ Open*, 7, 10.

Milbourne, L. (2005) Children, families and inter-agency work: Experiences of partnership work in primary education settings. *British Educational Research Journal*, 31, 6, 675–95.

Ministry of Housing Communities and Local Government (2019) *English Indices of Deprivation*, https://www.gov.uk/government/collections/english-indices-of-deprivation

Morris, K., Mason, W., Bywaters, P., Featherstone, B., Daniel, B., Brady, G., Hooper, J., Mirza, N., Scourfield, J. and Webb, C. (2018) Social work, poverty, and child welfare interventions. *Child and Family Social Work*, 23, 364–72.

Munro, E. (2011) *The Munro Review of Child Protection: Final Report*. London: Department for Education.

Nass, N. and Yen, C. (2010) *The Man Who Lied to His Laptop: What We Can Learn About Ourselves from Our Machines*. London: Current Publishing.

National Audit Office (2014a) *Academies and Maintained Schools: Oversight and Intervention*. London: National Audit Office.

National Audit Office (2014b) *Children in Care*. London: National Audit Office.

National Audit Office (2018a) *Converting Maintained Schools to Academies*. London: National Audit Office.

National Audit Office (2018b) *Financial Sustainability of Local Authorities*. London: National Audit Office.

National Crime Agency (NCA) (2018) *County Lines Drug Supply, Vulnerability and Harm*. London: NCA.

National Health Service Digital/Office of National Statistics (2018) *Mental Health of Children and Young People in England, 2017*, https://digital.nhs.uk/data-and-information/publications/statistical/mental-health-of-children-and-young-people-in-england/2017/2017

NSPCC (2020) *How Safe Are Our Children?* London: NSPCC.

Norgate, R., Traill, A. and Osbourne, C. (2009) Common Assessment Framework (CAF) – early views and issues. *Educational Psychology in Practice*, 25, 2, 139–50.

O'Connell, S. (2018) *Safeguarding Changes: Will They Make a Difference?* SecEd., https://www.sec-ed.co.uk/best-practice/safeguarding-changes-will-they-make-a-difference/

Ofcom (2018) *The Communications Market 2018*. London: Ofcom.

Office of Health Economics (1962) *Lives of Our Children: A Study of Childhood Mortality*. London: Office of Health Economics.

Office of Standards in Education (Ofsted) (2015a) *The Common Inspection Framework: Education, Skills and Early Years*. Manchester: Ofsted.

Office of Standards in Education (Ofsted) (2015b) *Early Help: Whose Responsibility?* Manchester: Ofsted.

Office of Standards in Education (Ofsted) (2017) *School Inspection Handbook*. Manchester: Ofsted.

Office of Standards in Education (Ofsted) (2019) *School Inspection Handbook*. Manchester: Ofsted.

Office of Standards in Education (Ofsted) (2021) *Review of Sexual Abuse in Schools and Colleges*. Manchester: Ofsted.

Office of Standards in Education (Ofsted), the Care Quality Commission (CQC), HMI Constabulary and Fire and Rescue Services (HMICFRS) and HMI Probation (HMIP) (2020) *The Multi-agency Response to Child Sexual Abuse in the Family Environment*. Manchester: Ofsted.

Oldfield, J., Hebron, J. and Humphrey, N. (2016) The role of school level protective factors in overcoming cumulative risk for behaviour difficulties in children with special educational needs and disabilities. *Psychology in the Schools*, 53, 8, 31–847.

Oliver, C., Statham, J. and Mooney, A. (2010) *Integrated Working: A Review of the Evidence*. Leeds: Children's Workforce Development Council.

Oxfordshire Safeguarding Board (2015) *Serious Case Review into Child Sexual Exploitation in Oxfordshire: From the Experiences of Children A, B, C, D, E, and F*, http://www.oscb.org.uk/wp-content/uploads/Serious-Case-Review-into-Child-Sexual-Exploitation-in-Oxfordshire-FINAL-Updated-14.3.15.pdf

Parton, N. (1991) *Governing the Family: Child Care, Child Protection and the State*. Basingstoke: Macmillan.

Parton, N. (2009) From Seebohm to *Think Family*: Reflections on 40 years of policy change of statutory children's social work in England. *Child and Family Social Work*, 14, 1, 68–78.

Parton, N. (2014) *The Politics of Child Protection*. Basingstoke: Palgrave Macmillan.

Parton, N. (2016) The contemporary politics of child protection: Part two (the BASPCAN founder's lecture 2015) *Child Abuse Review*, 25, 1, 9–16.

Parton, N. and Berridge, D. (2011) Child protection in England in N. Gilbert, N. Parton and M. Skivenes (eds) *Child Protection Systems*. Oxford: Oxford University Press.

Pearce, J. and Miller, C. (2020) Safeguarding children under Covid-19: What are we learning? *Journal of Children's Services*, 15, 4, 287–93, DOI: 10.1108/JCS-06-2020-0021

Pitchforth, J., Fahy, K., Ford, T., Wolpert, M., Viner, R. and Hargreaves, D. (2019) Mental health and well-being trends among children and young people in the UK, 1995–2014: Analysis of repeated cross-sectional national health surveys. *Psychological Medicine*, 49, 8, 1275–85.

Place2Be (2020) Huge rise in number of school-based counsellors over past three years, https://www.place2be.org.uk/media/rnuf5drw/place2be-and-naht-research-results.pdf

Pritchard, C., Cotton, A., Bowen, D. and Williams, R. (1998) A consumer study of young people's views on their education social worker: Engagement is a measure of an effective relationship. *British Journal of Social Work*, 28, 6, 915–38.

Puffett, N. (2010) Government confirms ban on Every Child Matters. *Children and Young People Now*, 9 August.

Purcell, C. (2020) *The Politics of Children's Services Reform: Re-examining Two Decades of Policy Change*. Bristol: Policy Press.

Ragin, C. (1987) *The Comparative Method*. Berkeley, CA: University of California Press.

Ragin, C. (2000) *Fuzzy-set Social Science*. Chicago, IL: University of Chicago Press.

Ragin, C., Drass, K. A. and Davey, S. (2006) *Fuzzy-Set/Qualitative Comparative Analysis 2.0*. Tucson, AZ: Department of Sociology, University of Arizona.

Rasasingham, R. (2015) The risk and protective factors of school absenteeism. *Open Journal of Psychiatry*, 5, 195–203.

Reid, K. (2008) The education welfare service: The case for a review in England. *Educational Studies*, 34, 3, 175–89.

Robinson, M. (1978) *Schools and Social Work*. London: Routledge and Kegan Paul.

Romanou, E. and Belton, E. (2020) Isolated and struggling: Social isolation and the risk of child maltreatment, in lockdown and beyond, NSPCC, https://learning.nspcc.org.uk/research-resources/2020/social-isolation-risk-child-abuse-during-and-after-coronavirus-pandemic

Rose, J. (1993) Willingly to school: The working-class response to elementary education in Britain, 1875–1918. *Journal of British Studies*, 32, 2, 114–38.

Rushmer, R. K. and Pallis, G. (2002) Inter-professional working: The wisdom of integrated working and the disaster of blurred boundaries. *Public Money and Management*, 23, 1, 59–66.

Ryan, M., Tunnard, J. and Brown, L. (2008) *Learning Development and Support Services Project. An Audit of the needs of 197 Children in Touch with Education Welfare Services in 4 Local Authority Areas*. London: Ryan, Tunnard and Brown.

Schneider, C. Q. and Claudius, W. (2010) Standards of good practice in qualitative comparative analysis (QCA) and fuzzy-sets. *Comparative Sociology*, 9, 3, 397–418.

Seebohm Committee (1968) *Report of the Committee on Local Authority and Allied Personal Social Services*. London: HMSO.

Sibieta, L. (2020) *2020 Annual Report on Education Spending in England: Schools*. London: Institute for Fiscal Studies.

Simpson, F. (2020) Five key things the Children's Minister told the Education Select Committee. *Children and Young People Now*, 22 April, https://www.cypnow.co.uk/news/article/five-key-things-the-children-s-minister-told-the-education-select-committee

Simpson, F. (2021) Arthur Labinjo-Hughes: Zahawi launches national review into murder of six-year-old. *Children and Young People Now*, 6 December, https://www.cypnow.co.uk/news/article/arthur-labinjo-hughes-zahawi-launches-national-review-into-murder-of-six-year-old

Social Care Institute for Excellence (2012) *Introduction to Children's Social Care*. London: Social Care Institute for Excellence.

Social Exclusion Unit (1998) *Truancy and School Exclusion*. London: Social Exclusion Unit.

Society of Education Officers (SEO) (1979) *The Education Welfare Service – A Reply to the ADSS Paper 'Social Work Services for Children in School'*. London: SEO.

Sosa, L. V., Cox, T. and Alvarez, M. (2016) *School Social Work: National Perspectives on Practice in Schools*. New York: Oxford University Press.

Spiker, P. (2000) *The Welfare State: A General Theory*. London: Sage.

Statham, J. (2011) *Working Together for Children: A Review of International Evidence on Interagency Working, to Inform the Development of Children's Services Committees in Ireland*. Dublin: Department of Children and Youth Affairs.

Stewart, W. and Clews, M. (2021) Sir Kevan Collins resigns over catch-up plan. *Times Education Supplement*, 2 June, https://www.tes.com/news/exclusive-sir-kevan-collins-resigns-over-covid-catch-up-schools-plan

Stokes, L., Dorsett, R., Manzoni, C., Runge, J. and Xu, L. (2021) *Supervision of Designated Safeguarding Leads in Primary Schools in Bolton*. London: What Works for Children's Social Care.

Tomlinson, K. (2003) *Effective Interagency Working: A Review of the Literature and Examples from Practice*. Slough: National Foundation for Educational Research.

Walsh, K. (2020) Complicating the Duality: Reconceptualising the Construction of Children in Victorian Child Protection Law. *Journal of Historical Sociology*, 33, 2, 263–77.

Webb, C. and Bywaters, P. (2018) Austerity, rationing and inequity: Trends in children's and young peoples' services expenditure in England between 2010 and 2015. *Local Government Studies*, 44, 1, 1–25.

Webster, R. (1991) Issues in school-based child sexual abuse prevention. *Children and Society*, 5, 2, 146–64.

Welshman, J. (1999) Evacuation, hygiene and social policy: The Our Towns Report of 1943. *The Historical Journal*, 42, 3, 781–807.

Williams, M. and Franklin, J. (2021) *Children and Young People's Services: Spending 2010–11 to 2019–20*. London: Children's Services Funding Alliance.

Williamson, G. (2021) *Education secretary speech to the Confederation of School Trusts*, 28 April, https://www.gov.uk/government/speeches/education-secretary-speech-to-the-confederation-of-school-trusts

Wilson, H. and Waddell, S. (2020) *Covid-19 and Early Intervention: Understanding the Impact, Preparing for Recovery*. London: Early Intervention Foundation.

Wilson, V. and Perrie, A. (2000) *Multidisciplinary Teamworking: Beyond the Barriers? A Review of the Issues*. Edinburgh: Scottish Council for Research in Education.

Wonnacott, J. (2012) *Mastering Social Work Supervision*. London: Jessica Kingsley.

Wood, A. (2016) *Wood Review of Local Safeguarding Children Boards*. London: Department for Education.

Wood, A. (2021) *Wood Report: Sector Expert Review of New Multi-agency Safeguarding Arrangements*. Department for Education, https://www.gov.uk/government/publications/wood-review-of-multi-agency-safeguarding-arrangements

Wright, S. (2009) The work of teachers and others in and around a Birmingham slum school 1891–1920. *History of Education*, 38, 6, 729–46.

Wright, S. (2012) Teachers, family and community in the urban elementary school: Evidence from English school log books *c*.1880–1918. *History of Education*, 41, 2, 155–73.

Yin, R. K. (2009) *Case Study Research, Design and Method*. 4th edition. London: Sage Publications Ltd.

Index

References to figures appear in *italic* type;
those in **bold** type refer to tables. References to endnotes
show the page and chapter number and the note number (152ch2n1).